LONGMAN LITERATURE

Equus

Peter Shaffer

Editor: Adrian Burke

LONGMAN

New Longman Literature
Post-1914 Fiction

Susan Hill *I'm the King of the Castle* 0 582 22173 0
          The Woman in Black 0 582 02660 1
          The Mist in the Mirror 0 582 25399 3
Aldous Huxley *Brave New World* 0 582 06016 8
Robin Jenks *The Cone-Gatherers* 0 582 06017 6
Doris Lessing *The Fifth Child* 0 582 06021 4
Joan Lindsay *Picnic at Hanging Rock* 0 582 08174 2
Bernard MacLaverty *Lamb* 0 582 06557 7
Brian Moore *Lies of Silence* 0 582 08170 X
George Orwell *Animal Farm* 0 582 06010 9
F Scott Fitzgerald *The Great Gatsby* 0 582 06023 0
Robert Swindells *Daz 4 Zoe* 0 582 30243 9
Anne Tyler *A Slipping-Down Life* 0 582 29247 6
Virginia Woolf *To the Lighthouse* 0 582 09714 2

Post-1914 Short Stories

Angelou, Goodison, Senior & Walker *Quartet of Stories* 0 582 28730 8
Stan Barstow *The Human Element and Other Stories* 0 582 23369 0
Roald Dahl *A Roald Dahl Selection* 0 582 22281 8
selected by Geoff Barton *Stories Old and New* 0 582 28931 9
selected by Madhu Bhinda *Stories from Africa* 0 582 25393 4
          Stories from Asia 0 582 03922 3
selected by Celeste Flower *Mystery and Horror* 0 582 28928 9
selected by Jane Christopher *War Stories* 0 582 28927 0
selected by Susan Hill *Ghost Stories* 0 582 02261 X
selected by Beverley Naidoo, *Global Tales* 0 582 28929 7
Christine Donovan & Alun Hicks
selected by Andrew Whittle & *Ten D H Lawrence Short Stories* 0 582 29249 2
Roy Blatchford

Post-1914 Poetry

collected & edited by Roy Blatchford *Voices of the Great War* 0 582 29248 4
edited by George Macbeth *Poetry 1900-1975* 0 582 35149 9
edited by Julia Markus & Paul Jordan *Poems 2* 0 582 25401 9

Post-1914 Plays

Alan Ayckbourn *Absent Friends* 0 582 30242 0
Terrence Rattigan *The Winslow Boy* 0 582 06019 2
Jack Rosenthal *P'Tang, Yang, Kipperbang and other TV Plays* 0 582 22389 X
Willy Russell *Educating Rita* 0 582 06013 3
          Shirley Valentine 0 582 08173 4
selected by Geoff Barton *Ten Short Plays* 0 582 25383 7
selected by Michael Marland *Scenes from Plays* 0 582 25394 2
Peter Shaffer *The Royal Hunt of the Sun* 0 582 06014 1
          Equus 0 582 09712 6
Bernard Shaw *Pygmalion* 0 582 06015 X
          Saint Joan 0 582 07786 9
Sheridan, Richard Brinsley *The Rivals/The School for Scandal* 0 582 25396 9

Contents

The writer on writing

I suppose my head has always been full of images.

Peter Shaffer is one of Britain's foremost contemporary dramatists. Born in 1926 and educated at Cambridge he had a variety of jobs before becoming a playwright. During the Second World War he worked down a coal-mine; he has also worked in the New York Public Library and as a journalist. He was awarded the CBE in the 1987 Birthday Honours List.

His first big success was with **Five Finger Exercise** in 1958, which ran for two years in London before transferring to New York. Other successes include **Amadeus** (which has been filmed), **The Private Ear: The Public Eye** and **The Royal Hunt of the Sun.** This last play represented a departure for Shaffer as a writer; he moved from detective stories, naturalistic drama and farce to epic theatre and the adoption of avant-garde stage techniques. It was while writing **The Royal Hunt of the Sun** that Shaffer first collaborated with the British theatrical director John Dexter, who also directed **Equus** in its first production at the National Theatre in 1973.

Both **The Royal Hunt of the Sun** and **Equus** are above all plays about faith. One of Shaffer's preoccupations as a writer is with the concept of worship and human beings' attempts at gaining or destroying a sense of religious faith. Another of his concerns is to do with the greyness, the absence of excitement and ecstasy in contemporary Britain which extends to its theatre. He has complained that English theatre 'deplores the large theme' and that it seems to prefer 'the minute fragment, minutely observed'. Shaffer's recent plays can be seen as a reaction to the dreariness and lack of passion which he sees in much drama. His plays are ambitious in their scope and what they require in order to be staged successfully. One stage direction in **The Royal Hunt of the Sun** simply reads: 'They climb the Andes.'

If it's a farce, let it be a big screaming farce. If it's an epic, let it be big. History. It's the tepidness of so much you see – I'd rather go to the pictures.

The Guardian, 8 August 1973

The Royal Hunt of the Sun was written before **Equus** and was first staged in 1964. Its success was largely due to the way Shaffer handled theatre action in a very physical manner; of this play he wrote: 'visual action is to me as much a part of the play as the dialogue'. Its subject matter was the conquest of Peru by Francisco Pizarro and it depicts the subjugation of 24 million Peruvians by 167 Spanish conquistadors. Shaffer examines the conflict between Pizarro and Atahuallpa, the Inca king, who are complete opposites in terms of their cultures. In common with **Equus** this earlier play offered the director the opportunity for spectacular staging. According to Shaffer,

It was a hugely lavish affair, superbly set and costumed . . . this sort of spectacle had not been seen on drab English stages for some while.

As in **Equus,** sound, light and movement were an essential part of the play. At different times the air would be filled with pulsating drumbeats, animal cries and ethnic music. The backdrop at the start of the play is a 'huge metal medallion, quartered by four black crucifixes, sharpened to resemble swords' out of which later is spilt a flood of 'blood red cloth' to represent massacre and bloodshed.

Amadeus, which came after **Equus**, shares with the other two plays what Shaffer sees as 'a common preoccupation with worship and man's attempts to acquire or murder a special divinity'. Of the three, only **Equus** has a contemporary setting although all have their basis in real historical events. **Amadeus** concerns the feud between Mozart and his arch-rival Salieri: the drama surrounds two very different protagonists, and once again Shaffer takes the opportunity to exploit the play's musical elements. Both **Equus** and **Amadeus** boast the rare distinction of having run for over a thousand performances on Broadway, and in 1984 **Amadeus** won the Academy Award for both script and film.

Shaffer's most recent plays are **Yonadab** and **Lettice and Lovage** which won the Evening Standard Drama Award for the best comedy of 1988.

Visual action has always been as important to Shaffer as the words. This is why it is so important for him to find the right director who can bring his mental images to life. Both *The Royal Hunt of the Sun* and *Equus* were originally staged by the same director, John Dexter, who seems to have had a particular ability to realise Shaffer's dramatic imagery in concrete terms. In *Equus* Shaffer and his director have to put on stage a mental world which can make comprehensible both an horrific deed and one man's reaction to it.

> *It is my object to tell tales; to conjure the spectres of horror and happiness, and fill other heads with the images which have haunted my own. My desire, I suppose, is to perturb and make gasp; to please and make laugh.*

If Peter Shaffer's plays often concern passion, it is perhaps because he is passionate about the physical work involved in producing a play. For him the journey from the original idea to its realisation by actors in front of an audience involves a labour of love. His is a restless spirit which carves away at a block of text until its final form is revealed in the manner of a sculptor. Shaffer has described the work of a playwright in terms which stress the craftsmanlike nature of his work: 'a man with hammer, hammering out a solid structure'.

Shaffer has said that all acts of creation are also 'acts of autobiography'. In fact, he has even confessed to having been known to ride himself 'but not obsessively. I'm not Alan Strang.' It might be argued that Shaffer's tireless work in continually re-shaping *Equus* until he found its ideal structure finds its counterpart within the play in the shape of Dysart's determination to follow his investigation of his patient and himself through to its bitter end. Shaffer has indeed declared himself interested in people who are passionately involved in the process of living and this explains his fascination with a boy who has blinded the animals he loves. 'I think that people who say "I'm an atheist" are rather boring. They've just stopped.'

Writing further about *Equus*, Shaffer observed:

> *Of all my plays Equus was the most private. I wrote it for myself. I had no notion how popular it was to become – its extraordinary run of well over a thousand performances on Broadway could never have been remotely envisaged by me.*

The play has been subject to a vast amount of commentary and misuse: a few doctors declaring it a madman's charter; some do-your-own-thingers using it as a means to justify every kind of human aberration. For me it is a deeply erotic play, and also one of tragic conflict. Tragedy obviously does not lie in a conflict of Right and Wrong, but in a collision between two different kinds of Right: in this case, surely, between Dysart's professional obligation to treat a terrified boy who has committed a dreadful crime, and Alan's passionate capacity for worship – his profound desire to cry 'O Magnum Mysterium!' alone in a rubbish-strewn field, his burning ecstasy set against his doctor's careful prosaicism. Dysart has to do what he does. Let no man say 'Do your own thing', for example, to Jack the Ripper. Yet in proceeding by his best and honourable lights, the doctor cannot but know that he is in some clear sense the destroyer of a passion he must forever, and rightly, envy.

Shaffer's genius as a dramatist lies in the ability to connect factual ideas to an emotional charge. Perhaps this is the reason for so many of his plays having their origins in fact: the Spanish conquest of Latin America; a boy blinding six horses; Mozart and his arch-rival. He has declared that he would like to do a play on the Faust legend, in which a man of great powers sells his soul to the devil. Such a theme ignites Shaffer's imagination because 'it's a question of what you give for what, and I don't mean money'. He challenges his audience's expectations about the theatre and he strives for 'an electricity sparked almost exclusively from the spoken word'.

Introduction

Equus has a strong narrative thrust; the audience is curious to know what drove Alan Strang to commit his hideous crime. The stage in *Equus* is literally haunted by spectral effigies of horses framing the action in a deliberately unrealistic manner. Shaffer is most insistent that the actors should avoid the 'cosy familiarity of a domestic animal'. His choice of language – direct, sparse, expletive-strewn – and his depiction of nudity and violence set out deliberately to shock.

Structure and form

The play's construction resembles that of the conventional detective story and thus betrays Shaffer's origins as a writer. The interest of the play is superficially an answer to the question: 'Why did the boy blind the horses?' However, the dramatic technique of having Dysart address a number of asides to the audience breaks the conventions of naturalistic drama and re-focuses our attention onto the psychiatrist.

The blinding of the horses is known from the very start of the play and so any dramatic tension will derive more from motive than from action. A revelatory process is one of the ways in which the drama unfolds itself as Dysart persuades Strang to re-enact the significant events from his childhood which lead up to the crime. This technique, similar to flashbacks in film, makes for strong, spare drama and also enables Dysart to perform the role of the chorus from classical drama. The play opens and closes in Dysart's office in a psychiatric hospital. One of the play's ironies is that Dysart is made to comment more on himself and his actions than on those of his patient.

The play's structure is a series of interviews, principally between Dysart and his patient. These are interspersed with monologues or asides to the audience where Dysart reflects upon the action and its effects on himself as a psychiatrist and as a man. Dysart dominates the play to such an extent that it really is almost a one-man show. Such a structure always poses the danger of becoming too abstract, too monotonous and lacking in action. Shaffer avoids such pitfalls by varying the modes of presentation: swift intercutting, asides, dialogue, enactment within the main play, the movement and the spectacle of the horse-figures; all such devices serve to provide variety, and alternately wind up and relax the dramatic tension of the play.

The role of psychiatry

Through Dysart, the play deals with the human need for worship and the search for meaning to life in an apparently godless universe. The loss of a certain, moral framework poses modern humanity the problem of how to judge its actions. Dysart sees the inadequacy of taking an exclusively psychological view when he is forced to admit the mystery of the human need for worship. This realisation drives Dysart to the point of breakdown.

> . . . Moments snap together like magnets, forging a chain of shackles. Why? I can trace them. I can even, with time, pull them apart again. But why at the start they ever magnetized at all – just those particular moments of experience and no others – I don't know. And nor does anyone else. Yet if I don't know – if I can never know that – then what am I doing here? . . .

Act 2, scene 22

Dysart emerges clearly as a Freudian psychiatrist. He encourages Alan to speak about his childhood and uncovers the family setting which repressed his early religious and sexual impulses. He is interested in Alan's dreams and feels he has 'understood' him once he has got to the root of his sexual obsession with horses. His main method involves the psychiatrist in observing how Alan thinks and by interpreting his dreams. This process forces Alan to re-live the significant events from his childhood which contributed to his later emotional disorder.

The Freudian interpretation of human beings' deepest impulses raises but does not answer the basic question about the human capacity for evil. Dysart views Alan's personality as being the result of his childhood influences. By this account Alan is neither mad nor evil but the product of his environment. This is a view which Dora, Alan's mother challenges:

> ... *Whatever's happened has happened* because of Alan. *Alan is himself. Every soul is itself. If you added up everything we ever did to him, from his first day on earth to this, you wouldn't find why he did this terrible thing – because that's* him: *not just all of our things added up ... I only know he was my Alan, and then the Devil came.*

Act 2, scene 23

Characterisation

The play has been criticised for the two-dimensional nature of the supporting characters. Dr Dysart dominates the play by his very presence throughout and by his control over the narration and the patient. There is never any suggestion that he is untypical of his profession. Dr Dysart does not stop at analysing his patient; he explains himself. He analyses his marriage and berates himself for its failure; he goes on to condemn himself for not simply taking up the cult of the primitive which he toys with while on holiday in Greece. In contrast, Alan's childhood in a social vacuum is briefly sketched through acted flashback and by statements collected from key witnesses.

The other characters can appear as cardboard roles or little more than types. For example, to what extent do we believe in Frank and Dora Strang? It is arguable that beyond being stereotypes of lower-middle-class parents they only need to be there to 'explain' Alan's repressed childhood and later neurosis. If we are really to believe in family pressures as the chief source of Alan's disturbance then the relationship between Frank and Dora requires much more profound and subtle examination.

Dalton and the Young Horseman are even more obviously 'horsy' types whom Shaffer seems to hold in particular contempt. Hesther Salomon is the only character – apart from Alan – who moves in the real world of Dysart's consulting room but she is usually no more than a sounding board for the psychiatrist's confessions. Would the play have been radically different if these had been addressed to the audience, like Dysart's other asides? It might be argued that Jill exists purely as an 'Eve' character to seduce Alan from his 'Eden' of the stable.

Passion and religion

Passion rather than religion is perhaps the real subject of **Equus**. Dysart broods over the failure of his marriage which lacks the naked, animal passion of Alan's relationship with Jill. Alan's parents' marriage is a pretty sterile affair with Frank sloping off to see dirty films for some small sexual gratification.

By comparison Shaffer characterises Jill's relationship with Alan in terms of naturalness and caring. Sex between the two young people is seen as the natural and fitting fulfilment of their courtship. Jill is the one person who seems to have no 'hang-ups' about sex. Being with horses is also seen as a way of gaining satisfaction from the world. 'Just have fun,' Dalton tells Alan when he takes him on.

Critical reaction to the play

When **Equus** was first produced it shocked the critics and its audiences. Its shock lay in its message about the world which western man has built for himself: a world which is flat and lacking in passion and which for most of us is the controlled mediocrity of suburban life. It is better, says Shaffer, to worship some god than none, even if the passion aroused may turn to violence. The atheist, puritanical father is discovered surreptitiously visiting a 'dirty film'. Shaffer implies that it is better to risk all in the way that Alan does, than to reduce the glories of sexual passion to squalid, solitary fumblings beneath a raincoat.

> *He* [Alan] *lives* one hour *every three weeks – howling in a mist. And after the service kneels to a slave who stands over him obviously and unthrowably his master. With my body I thee worship!* . . .

Act 2, scene 25

Critical reaction has not always been favourable. More than one critic has found fault with the play's construction: feeling that the neatness and logic with which Shaffer's Dr Dysart solves his case destroy our belief and undermine the play's special pleading for passion.

What was recognised from the outset is the power of the play as a piece of theatre. The reaction of **The Observer**'s theatre critic is typical: 'Taken realistically the play is a dud. . . . Theatrically it is a triumph.' The intensity of the images dreamed up by Shaffer, where the actors paw the ground in silver masks, horse and rider combined, serve to tell the audience all they need to know about the boy's obsession. Indeed, there is more than mere spectacle to the detailed realisation for the play's staging which Shaffer provides in his Author's notes on the play (page xxi). They serve as a precise instrument for the generation of dramatic tension.

The writing of *Equus*

Shaffer's first draft was very much concerned with the blinding of the horses and an attempt to explain this act. The character of Dysart, the psychiatrist, had only just started to emerge and Shaffer was encouraged by the director, John Dexter, to explore this character more deeply.

Shaffer now embarked on the process of writing and destroying his writing and re-writing, often revising his work in the light of criticism and instruction from the director.

> *One never ends really. It's not just a text, sacred words written down. The play is animated in rehearsal. I don't think the role of a playwright ever ends, not even after the first night.*

Peter Shaffer in an interview in **The Guardian,** 8 August 1973

Both writer and director decided on a structure which 'cut across time illogically' to make the events clear and not to attempt a chronological narration which an orthodox play might do. This led Shaffer to the first image of a boy caressing a horse with which the play opens.

> *Darkness.*
>> *Silence.*
>> *Dim light up on the square. In a spotlight stands Alan Strang, a lean boy of seventeen in sweater and jeans. In front of him, the horse Nugget. Alan's pose represents a contour of great tenderness: his head is pressed against the shoulder of the horse, his hands stretching up to fondle its head.*

During the re-writing Shaffer developed further the characters of Alan's parents. Originally, both father and mother had been depicted as being deeply religious but it suited the purpose of the play to change Frank into an atheist, thus heightening dramatic conflict.

The greatest change during re-writing was one of emphasis. The play's focus moved away from the boy to concentrate instead on his effect on his analyst. In Act 1 Dysart finds himself profoundly affected by his contact with Alan Strang and in Act 2 he comes to realise the inadequacy of his psychiatric skills. Peter Shaffer wrote:

> . . . *the play, as it grew under my hands, came more and more to question the ultimate uses of psychiatry. In the first draft the doctor was drawn more vaguely; less in the central position. In the second draft he grew more prominent, and his self-doubts more important to the meaning of the play.*

For the play to succeed fully, writer and director were agreed that its climax had to be a verbal one where Dysart expressed the crisis which was inside his own head. The set design reflected the desire to put Dysart on trial, to expose him totally in all his aspects to the audience. Both audience and cast were placed in a witness box or an operating theatre where they could concentrate upon the spectacle of a rational man realising that he no longer has any control over events.

During the writing process the play became for Shaffer not only a 'deeply erotic play' but also one of 'tragic conflict'. The play concludes by confronting Dysart with an insoluble dilemma. Until he accepts the

☐ Reading log

One of the easiest ways of keeping track of your reading is to keep a log book. This can be any exercise book or folder that you have to hand, but make sure that you reserve it exclusively for reflecting on your reading.

After every reading session, write an entry in your reading log using the following headings as a guide.

- *Discussion/prediction*

  Is there anything which puzzles you? Note down any questions you might want to discuss with friends or with your teacher. Try to predict what will happen next and later record how close you were in your predictions. Also, make a note of the clues in the text which influenced your predictions.

- *Character study*

  To help you keep track of each character and the part they play, open up a page for each of the main characters in the play. Note down:
  - the part they play in each scene;
  - any aspects they reveal of their character;
  - relevant comments made by them or by other characters;
  - changes or developments in character.

  What is your attitude to the character? Does it change during the course of the play?

- *Dramatic significance*

  Briefly summarise:
  - the action of each scene;
  - characters involved;
  - setting and plot development (show how your total knowledge of the play has been added to).

  Also, make a note of the means by which the playwright has presented the material, for example through dialogue, re-enactment, confrontation, and so on.

- *Themes*

  For each scene make notes on the introduction and development of the main themes in the play. Say what you think the attitude of the playwright is to each theme. Are different characters used to express different views of the theme?

- *Language*

  What kinds of language does the writer use? Are characters shown to be different from one another by the way in which they speak? Is the language colloquial or poetic? Do characters ever speak in asides or directly address the audience?

  Consider the reasons for the writer's use of language.

Equus

Author's note on the book

What appears in this book is a description of the first production of *Equus* at the National Theatre in July 1973. In making this description, I am partly satisfying myself, but also partly bowing to demand.

When people buy the published text of a new play, they mostly want to recall the experience they received in the theatre. That experience is composed, of course, not merely of the words they heard, but the gestures they saw, and the lighting, and the look of the thing.

There are, however, evils attendant on this sort of description. It can imprison a play in one particular stylization. Just as seriously, it can do a real injustice to the original Director, by incorporating his ideas without truly acknowledging them. Worse, if the Director is as inventive as John Dexter, it can actually seem to minimise those ideas, just by flatly setting down on paper what was far from flat on the stage, and listing inexpressively details of his work which, in accumulation, became deeply expressive.

Dexter directs powerfully through suggestion. Into the theatrical spaces he contrives, flows the communal imagination of an audience. He enables it to charge the action of a play with electric life. He is a master of gesture and of economy. Aesthetically, his founding fathers are Noh Drama and Bertholt Brecht: the plain plank; the clear light; the great pleasure in a set-piece. I do not mean by this that he would ever direct a single minute of physical action which detracted from the meaning of a play, or in some grand visual sense subverted it – he sharply dislikes effect isolated from context – but he is naturally and rightly drawn to plays which demand elaborate physical actions to complete them.

The Royal Hunt of the Sun and *Black Comedy*, both of which he directed, are such pieces: and so is *Equus*. Their visual action is to me as much a part of the play as the dialogue. I suppose my head has always been full of images. The gold masks staring hopefully and then in gathering despair at the sky, at the end of *The Royal Hunt of the Sun*, had been part of my imagination ever since I first saw a Peruvian funeral mask with its elongated eyes and red-smeared cheeks. Brindsley Miller in the lit-up darkness of *Black Comedy*, slowly moving the spiky legs of a Regency chair one inch before the innocent face of his spinster neighbour, had tiptoed that very journey in my head as I sat at my desk. But such images, like the Field of Ha Ha in *Equus* with its mist and nettles, still have to be externalized. In John Dexter's courageous and precise staging, they acquire a vibrant and unforgettable life.

While I am confessing debts, let me mention John Napier who created the tough, bright masks of horsedom; Andy Phillips who lit them superbly; and above all, Claude Chagrin, who animated them. She created, with the help of six human actors, a stable of Superhorses to stalk through the mind.

Finally, out of a fine company I must set down the names of three actors who made the first performance of this play live with a very special intensity. Alec McCowen's *Dysart* touched audiences deeply with its dry agony. Peter Firth's *Alan* left them sighing with admiration. Nicholas Clay's horse, *Nugget* was, quite simply, unforgettable.

Rehearsing a play is making the word flesh. Publishing a play is reversing the process. I can only hope this book is not too unjust to these brilliant people.

Author's notes on the play

One weekend over two years ago, I was driving with a friend through bleak countryside. We passed a stable. Suddenly he was reminded by it of an alarming crime which he had heard about recently at a dinner party in London. He knew only one horrible detail, and his complete mention of it could barely have lasted a minute – but it was enough to arouse in me an intense fascination.

The act had been committed several years before by a highly disturbed young man. It had deeply shocked a local bench of magistrates. It lacked, finally, any coherent explanation.

A few months later my friend died. I could not verify what he had said, or ask him to expand it. He had given me no name, no place, and no time. I don't think he knew them. All I possessed was his report of a dreadful event, and the feeling it engendered in me. I knew very strongly that I wanted to interpret it in some entirely personal way. I had to create a mental world in which the deed could be made comprehensible.

Every person and incident in *Equus* is of my own invention, save the crime itself: and even that I modified to accord with what I feel to be acceptable theatrical proportion. I am grateful now that I have never received confirmed details of the real story, since my concern has been more and more with a different kind of exploration.

I have been lucky, in doing final work on the play, to have enjoyed the advice and expert comment of a distinguished child psychiatrist. Through him I have tried to keep things real in a more naturalistic sense. I have also come to perceive that psychiatrists are an immensely varied breed, professing immensely varied methods and techniques. Martin Dysart is simply one doctor in one hospital. I must take responsibility for him, as I do for his patient.

The set

A square of wood set on a circle of wood.

The square resembles a railed boxing ring. The rail, also of wood, encloses three sides. It is perforated on each side by an opening. Under the rail are a few vertical slats, as if in a fence. On the downstage side there is no rail. The whole square is set on ball bearings, so that by slight pressure from actors standing round it on the circle, it can be made to turn round smoothly by hand.

On the square are set three little plain benches, also of wood. They are placed parallel with the rail, against the slats, but can be moved out by the actors to stand at right angles to them.

Set into the floor of the square, and flush with it, is a thin metal pole, about a yard high. This can be raised out of the floor, to stand upright. It acts as a support for the actor playing Nugget, when he is ridden.

In the area outside the circle stand benches. Two downstage left and right, are curved to accord with the circle. The left one is used by Dysart as a listening and observing post when he is out of the square, and also by Alan as his hospital bed. The right one is used by Alan's parents, who sit side by side on it. (Viewpoint is from the main body of the audience.)

Further benches stand upstage, and accommodate the other actors. All the cast of *Equus* sits on stage the entire evening. They get up to perform their scenes, and return when they are done to their places around the set. They are witnesses, assistants – and especially a Chorus.

Upstage, forming a backdrop to the whole, are tiers of seats in the fashion of a dissecting theatre, formed into two railed-off blocks, pierced by a central tunnel. In these blocks sit members of the audience. During the play, Dysart addresses them directly from time to time, as he addresses the main body of the theatre. No other actor ever refers to them.

To left and right, downstage, stand two ladders on which are suspended horse masks.

The colour of all benches is olive green.

Above the stage hangs a battery of lights, set in a huge metal ring. Light cues, in this version, will be only of the most general description.

The horses

The actors wear track-suits of chestnut velvet. On their feet are light strutted hooves, about four inches high, set on metal horse-shoes. On their hands are gloves of the same colour. On their heads are tough masks made of alternating bands of silver wire and leather: their eyes are outlined by leather blinkers. The actors' own heads are seen beneath them: no attempt should be made to conceal them.

Any literalism which could suggest the cosy familiarity of a domestic animal – or worse, a pantomime horse – should be avoided. The actors should never crouch on all fours, or even bend forward. They must always – except on the one occasion where Nugget is ridden – stand upright, as if the body of the horse extended invisibly behind them. Animal effect must be created entirely mimetically, through the use of legs, knees, neck, face, and the turn of the head which can move the mask above it through all the gestures of equine wariness and pride. Great care must also be taken that the masks are put on before the audience with very precise timing – the actors watching each other, so that the masking has an exact and ceremonial effect.

The Chorus

References are made in the text to the Equus Noise. I have in mind a choric effect, made by all the actors sitting round upstage, and composed of humming, thumping, and stamping – though never of neighing or whinnying. This Noise heralds or illustrates the presence of Equus the God.

Characters

MARTIN DYSART, *a psychiatrist*
ALAN STRANG
FRANK STRANG, *his father*
DORA STRANG, *his mother*
HESTHER SALOMON, *a magistrate*
JILL MASON
HARRY DALTON, *a stable owner*
A YOUNG HORSEMAN
A NURSE

Six actors – *including the Young Horseman, who also plays Nugget – appear as Horses.*

The main action of the play takes place in Rokeby Psychiatric Hospital in Southern England.

The time is the present.

The play is divided into numbered scenes, indicating a change of time or locale or mood. The action, however, is continuous.

Act One

1

Darkness.

Silence.

Dim light up on the square. In a spotlight stands Alan Strang, a lean boy of seventeen, in sweater and jeans. In front of him, the horse Nugget. Alan's pose represents a contour of great tenderness: his head is pressed against the shoulder of the horse, his hands stretching up to fondle its head. The horse in turn nuzzles his neck.

The flame of a cigarette lighter jumps in the dark. Lights come up slowly on the circle. On the left bench, downstage, Martin Dysart, smoking. A man in his mid-forties.

DYSART With one particular horse, called Nugget, he embraces. The animal digs its sweaty brow into his cheek, and they stand in the dark for an hour – like a necking couple. And of all nonsensical things – I keep thinking about the *horse*! Not the boy: the horse, and what it may be trying to do. I keep seeing that huge head kissing him with its chained mouth. Nudging through the metal some desire absolutely irrelevant to filling its belly or propagating its own kind. What desire could that be? Not to stay a horse any longer? Not to remain reined up for ever in those particular genetic strings? Is it possible, at certain moments we cannot imagine, a horse can add its sufferings together – the non-stop jerks and jabs that are its daily life – and turn them into grief? What use is grief to a horse?

Alan leads Nugget out of the square and they disappear together up the tunnel, the horse's hooves scraping delicately on the wood.

Dysart rises, and addresses both the large audience in the theatre and the smaller one on stage.

You see, I'm lost. What use, I should be asking, are questions like these to an overworked psychiatrist in a provincial hospital? They're worse than useless: they are, in fact, subversive.

He enters the square. The light grows brighter.

The thing is, I'm desperate. You see, I'm wearing that horse's head myself. That's the feeling. All reined up in old language and old assumptions, straining to jump clean-hoofed on to a whole new track of being I only suspect is there. I can't see it, because my educated, average head is being held at the wrong angle. I can't jump because the bit forbids it, and my own basic force – my horsepower, if you like – is too little. The only thing I know for sure is this: a horse's head is finally unknowable to me. Yet I handle children's heads – which I must presume to be more complicated, at least in the area of my chief concern. . . . In a way, it has nothing to do with this boy. The doubts have been there for years, piling up steadily in this dreary place. It's only the extremity of this case that's made them active. I know that. The *extremity* is the point! All the same, whatever the reason, they are now, these doubts, not just vaguely worrying – but intolerable . . . I'm sorry. I'm not making much sense. Let me start properly: in order. It began one Monday last month, with Hesther's visit.

2

The light gets warmer.
He sits. Nurse enters the square.

NURSE Mrs Salomon to see you, Doctor.
DYSART Show her in, please.
Nurse leaves and crosses to where Hesther sits.

Some days I blame Hesther. She brought him to me. But of course that's nonsense. What is he but a last straw? A last symbol? If it hadn't been him, it would have been the next patient, or the next. At least, I suppose so.

Hesther enters the square: a woman in her mid-forties.

HESTHER Hallo, Martin.

Dysart rises and kisses her on the cheek.

DYSART Madam Chairman! Welcome to the torture chamber!

HESTHER It's good of you to see me right away.

DYSART You're a welcome relief. Take a couch.

HESTHER It's been a day?

DYSART No – just a fifteen year old schizophrenic, and a girl of eight thrashed into catatonia by her father. Normal, really . . . You're in a state.

HESTHER Martin, this is the most shocking case I ever tried.

DYSART So you said on the phone.

HESTHER I mean it. My bench wanted to send the boy to prison. For life, if they could manage it. It took me two hours solid arguing to get him sent to you instead.

DYSART Me?

HESTHER I mean, to hospital.

DYSART Now look, Hesther. Before you say anything else, I can take no more patients at the moment. I can't even cope with the ones I have.

HESTHER You must.

DYSART Why?

HESTHER Because most people are going to be disgusted by the whole thing. Including doctors.

DYSART May I remind you I share this room with two highly competent psychiatrists?

HESTHER Bennett and Thoroughgood. They'll be as shocked as the public.

DYSART That's an absolutely unwarrantable statement.

HESTHER Oh, they'll be cool and exact. And underneath they'll be revolted, and immovably English. Just like my bench.

DYSART Well, what am I? Polynesian?

HESTHER You know exactly what I mean! . . . (*pause*) Please, Martin. It's vital. You're this boy's only chance.

DYSART Why? What's he done? Dosed some little girl's Pepsi

3

with Spanish Fly? What could possibly throw your bench
into two-hour convulsions?

HESTHER He blinded six horses with a metal spike.

A long pause.

DYSART Blinded?

HESTHER Yes.

DYSART All at once, or over a period?

HESTHER All on the same night.

DYSART Where?

HESTHER In a riding stable near Winchester. He worked there
at weekends.

DYSART How old?

HESTHER Seventeen.

DYSART What did he say in Court?

HESTHER Nothing. He just sang.

DYSART Sang?

HESTHER Any time anyone asked him anything.

Pause.

Please take him, Martin. It's the last favour I'll ever ask
you.

DYSART No, it's not.

HESTHER No, it's not – and he's probably abominable. All I
know is, he needs you badly. Because there really is nobody
within a hundred miles of your desk who can handle him.
And perhaps understand what this is about. Also....

DYSART What?

HESTHER There's something very special about him.

DYSART In what way?

HESTHER Vibrations.

DYSART You and your vibrations.

HESTHER They're quite startling. You'll see.

DYSART When does he get here?

HESTHER Tomorrow morning. Luckily there was a bed in
Neville Ward. I know this is an awful imposition, Martin.
Frankly I didn't know what else to do.

Pause.

DYSART Can you come in and see me on Friday?

HESTHER Bless you!

DYSART If you come after work I can give you a drink. Will 6.30 be all right?

HESTHER You're a dear. You really are.

DYSART Famous for it.

HESTHER Goodbye.

DYSART By the way, what's his name?

HESTHER Alan Strang.

She leaves and returns to her seat.

DYSART (*to audience*) What did I expect of him? Very little, I promise you. One more dented little face. One more adolescent freak. The usual unusual. One great thing about being in the adjustment business: you're never short of customers.

Nurse comes down the tunnel, followed by Alan. She enters the square.

NURSE Alan Strang, Doctor.

The boy comes in.

DYSART Hallo. My name's Martin Dysart. I'm pleased to meet you.

He puts out his hand. Alan does not respond in any way.

That'll be all, Nurse, thank you.

3

Nurse goes out and back to her place. Dysart sits, opening a file.

So: did you have a good journey? I hope they gave you lunch at least. Not that there's much to choose between a British Rail meal and one here.

Alan stands staring at him.

DYSART Won't you sit down?

Pause. He does not. Dysart consults his file.

Is this your full name? Alan Strang?

Silence.

And you're seventeen. Is that right? Seventeen? ... Well?

ALAN (*singing low*) Double your pleasure
　　Double your fun
　　With Doublemint, Doublemint
　　Doublemint gum.

DYSART (*unperturbed*) Now, let's see. You work in an electrical shop during the week. You live with your parents, and your father's a printer. What sort of things does he print?

ALAN (*singing louder*) Double your pleasure
　　Double your fun
　　With Doublemint, Doublemint
　　Doublemint gum.

DYSART I mean does he do leaflets and calendars? Things like that?

The boy approaches him, hostile.

ALAN (*singing*) Try the taste of Martini
　　The most beautiful drink in the world.
　　It's the right one –
　　The bright one –
　　That's Martini!

DYSART I wish you'd sit down, if you're going to sing. Don't you think you'd be more comfortable?

Pause.

ALAN (*singing*) There's only one T in Typhoo!
　　In packets and in teabags too.
　　Any way you make it, you'll find it's true:
　　There's only one T in Typhoo!

DYSART (*appreciatively*) Now that's a good song. I like it better than the other two. Can I hear that one again?

Alan starts away from him, and sits on the upstage bench.

ALAN (*singing*) Double your pleasure
　　Double your fun
　　With Doublemint, Doublemint
　　Doublemint gum.

DYSART (*smiling*) You know I was wrong. I really do think that one's better. It's got such a catchy tune. Please do that one again.

Silence. The boy glares at him.

I'm going to put you in a private bedroom for a little while. There are one or two available, and they're rather more pleasant than being in a ward. Will you please come and see me tomorrow? ... (*He rises*) By the way, which parent is it who won't allow you to watch television? Mother or father? Or is it both? (*calling out of the door*) Nurse!

Alan stares at him. Nurse comes in.

NURSE Yes, Doctor?

DYSART Take Strang here to Number Three, will you? He's moving in there for a while.

NURSE Very good, Doctor.

DYSART (*to Alan*) You'll like that room. It's nice.

The boy sits staring at Dysart. Dysart returns the stare.

NURSE Come along, young man. This way.... I said this way, please.

Reluctantly Alan rises and goes to Nurse, passing dangerously close to Dysart, and out through the left door. Dysart looks after him, fascinated.

4

Nurse and patient move on to the circle, and walk downstage to the bench where the doctor first sat, which is to serve also as Alan's bed.

NURSE Well now: isn't this nice? You're lucky to be in here, you know, rather than the ward. That ward's a noisy old place.

ALAN (*singing*) Let's go where you wanna go – Texaco!

NURSE (*contemplating him*) I hope you're not going to make a nuisance of yourself. You'll have a much better time of it here, you know, if you behave yourself.

ALAN Fuck off.

NURSE (*tight*) That's the bell there. The lav's down the corridor.

She leaves him, and goes back to her place. Alan lies down.

5

Dysart stands in the middle of the square and addresses the audience. He is agitated.

DYSART That night, I had this very explicit dream. In it I'm a chief priest in Homeric Greece. I'm wearing a wide gold mask, all noble and bearded, like the so-called Mask of Agamemnon found at Mycenae. I'm standing by a thick round stone and holding a sharp knife. In fact, I'm officiating at some immensely important ritual sacrifice, on which depends the fate of the crops or of a military expedition. The sacrifice is a herd of children: about five hundred boys and girls. I can see them stretching away in a long queue, right across the plain of Argos. I know it's Argos because of the red soil. On either side of me stand two assistant priests, wearing masks as well: lumpy, pop-eyed masks, such as also were found at Mycenae. They are enormously strong, these other priests, and absolutely tireless. As each child steps forward, they grab it from behind and throw it over the stone. Then, with a surgical skill which amazes even me, I fit in the knife and slice elegantly down to the navel, just like a seamstress following a pattern. I part the flaps, sever the inner tubes, yank them out and throw them hot and steaming on to the floor. The other two then study the pattern they make, as if they were reading hieroglyphics. It's obvious to me that I'm tops as chief priest. It's this unique talent for carving that has got me where I am. The only thing is, unknown to them, I've started to feel distinctly nauseous. And with each victim, it's getting worse. My face is going green behind the mask. Of course, I redouble my efforts to look professional – cutting and snipping for all I'm worth: mainly because I know that if ever those two assistants so much as glimpse my distress – and the implied doubt that this repetitive and smelly work is doing any social good at all – I will be the next across the stone. And then, of course – the damn mask begins to slip. The priests both turn and look at it – it slips some more – they see the green sweat running down my face – their gold pop-eyes suddenly fill up with blood – they tear the knife out of my hand ... and I wake up.

6

Hesther enters the square. Light grows warmer.

HESTHER That's the most indulgent thing I ever heard.

DYSART You think?

HESTHER Please don't be ridiculous. You've done the most superb work with children. You must know that.

DYSART Yes, but do the children?

HESTHER Really!

DYSART I'm sorry.

HESTHER So you should be.

DYSART I don't know why you listen. It's just professional menopause. Everyone gets it sooner or later. Except you.

HESTHER Oh, of course. I feel totally fit to be a magistrate all the time.

DYSART No, you don't – but then that's you feeling unworthy to fill a job. I feel the job is unworthy to fill me.

HESTHER Do you seriously?

DYSART More and more. I'd like to spend the next ten years wandering very slowly around the *real* Greece ... Anyway, all this dream nonsense is your fault.

HESTHER Mine?

DYSART It's that lad of yours who started it off. Do you know it's his face I saw on every victim across the stone?

HESTHER Strang?

DYSART He has the strangest stare I ever met.

HESTHER Yes.

DYSART It's exactly like being accused. Violently accused. But

9

what of? . . . Treating him is going to be unsettling. Especially in my present state. His singing was direct enough. His speech is more so.

HESTHER (*surprised*) He's talking to you, then?

DYSART Oh yes. It took him two more days of commercials, and then he snapped. Just like that – I suspect it has something to do with his nightmares.

Nurse walks briskly round the circle, a blanket over her arm, a clipboard of notes in her hand.

HESTHER He has nightmares?

DYSART Bad ones.

NURSE We had to give him a sedative or two, Doctor. Last night it was exactly the same.

DYSART (*to Nurse*) What does he do? Call out?

NURSE (*to desk*) A lot of screaming, Doctor.

DYSART (*to Nurse*) Screaming?

NURSE One word in particular.

DYSART (*to Nurse*) You mean a special word?

NURSE Over and over again. (*consulting clipboard*) It sounds like 'Ek'.

HESTHER Ek?

NURSE Yes, Doctor. Ek . . . 'Ek!' he goes. 'Ek!'

HESTER How weird.

NURSE When I woke him up he clung to me like he was going to break my arm.

She stops at Alan's bed. He is sitting up. She puts the blanket over him, and returns to her place.

DYSART And then he burst in – just like that – without knocking or anything. Fortunately, I didn't have a patient with me.

ALAN (*jumping up*) Dad!

HESTHER What?

DYSART The answer to a question I'd asked him two days before. Spat out with the same anger as he sang the commercials.

HESTHER Dad what?

ALAN Who hates telly.

He lies downstage on the circle, as if watching television.

HESTHER You mean his dad forbids him to watch?

DYSART Yes.

ALAN It's a dangerous drug.

HESTHER Oh, really!

Frank stands up and enters the scene downstage on the circle. A man in his fifties.

FRANK (*to Alan*) It may not look like that, but that's what it is. Absolutely fatal mentally, if you receive my meaning.

Dora follows him on. She is also middle-aged.

DORA That's a little extreme, dear, isn't it?

FRANK You sit in front of that thing long enough, you'll become stupid for life – like most of the population. (*to Alan*) The thing is, it's a *swiz*. It seems to be offering you something, but actually it's taking something away. Your intelligence and your concentration, every minute you watch it. That's a true swiz, do you see?

Seated on the floor, Alan shrugs.

I don't want to sound like a spoilsport, old chum – but there really is no substitute for reading. What's the matter: don't you like it?

ALAN It's all right.

FRANK I know you think it's none of my beeswax, but it really is you know ... Actually, it's a disgrace when you come to think of it. You the son of a printer, and never opening a book! If all the world was like you, I'd be out of a job, if you receive my meaning!

DORA All the same, times change, Frank.

FRANK (*reasonably*) They change if you let them change, Dora. Please return that set in the morning.

ALAN (*crying out*) No!

DORA Frank! No!

FRANK I'm sorry, Dora, but I'm not having that thing in the house a moment longer. I told you I didn't want it to begin with.

11

DORA But, dear, everyone watches television these days!

FRANK Yes, and what do they watch? Mindless violence! Mindless jokes! Every five minutes some laughing idiot selling you something you don't want, just to bolster up the economic system. (*to Alan*) I'm sorry, old chum.

He leaves the scene and sits again in his place.

HESTHER He's a Communist, then?

DYSART Old-type Socialist, I'd say. Relentlessly self-improving.

HESTHER They're *both* older than you'd expect.

DYSART So I gather.

DORA (*looking after Frank*) Really, dear, you are very extreme!

She leaves the scene too, and again sits beside her husband.

HESTHER She's an ex-school teacher, isn't she?

DYSART Yes. The boy's proud of that. We got on to it this afternoon.

ALAN (*belligerently, standing up*) She knows more than you.

Hesther crosses and sits by Dysart. During the following, the boy walks round the circle, speaking to Dysart but not looking at him. Dysart replies in the same manner.

DYSART (*to Alan*) Does she?

ALAN I bet I do too. I bet I know more history than you.

DYSART (*to Alan*) Well, I bet you don't.

ALAN All right: who was the Hammer of the Scots?

DYSART (*to Alan*) I don't know: who?

ALAN King Edward the First. Who never smiled again?

DYSART (*to Alan*) I don't know: who?

ALAN You don't know anything, do you? It was Henry the First. I know all the Kings.

DYSART (*to Alan*) And who's your favourite?

ALAN John.

DYSART (*to Alan*) Why?

ALAN Because he put out the eyes of that smarty little –

Pause.

(*sensing he has said something wrong*) Well, he didn't really. He was prevented, because the gaoler was merciful!

12

HESTHER Oh dear.

ALAN *He was prevented!*

DYSART Something odder was to follow.

ALAN Who said 'Religion is the opium of the people'?

HESTHER Good Lord!

Alan giggles.

DYSART The odd thing was, he said it with a sort of guilty snigger. The sentence is obviously associated with some kind of tension.

HESTHER What did you say?

DYSART I gave him the right answer. (*to Alan*) Karl Marx.

ALAN No.

DYSART (*to Alan*) Then who?

ALAN Mind your own beeswax.

DYSART It's probably his dad. He may say it to provoke his wife.

HESTHER And you mean she's religious?

DYSART She could be. I tried to discover – none too successfully.

ALAN Mind your own beeswax!

Alan goes back to bed and lies down in the dark.

DYSART However, I shall find out on Sunday.

HESTHER What do you mean?

DYSART (*getting up*) I want to have a look at his home, so I invited myself over.

HESTHER Did you?

DYSART If there's any tension over religion, it should be evident on a Sabbath evening! I'll let you know.

He kisses her cheek and they part, both leaving the square. Hesther sits in her place again; Dysart walks round the circle, and greets Dora who stands waiting for him downstage.

7

DYSART (*shaking hands*) Mrs Strang.

DORA Mr Strang's still at the Press, I'm afraid. He should be home in a minute.

DYSART He works Sundays as well?

DORA Oh, yes. He doesn't set much store by Sundays.

DYSART Perhaps you and I could have a little talk before he comes in.

DORA Certainly. Won't you come into the living room?

She leads the way into the square. She is very nervous.

Please . . . .

She motions him to sit, then holds her hands tightly together.

DYSART Mrs Strang, have you any idea how this thing could have occurred?

DORA I can't imagine, Doctor. It's all so unbelievable! . . . Alan's always been such a gentle boy. He loves animals! Especially horses.

DYSART Especially?

DORA Yes. He even has a photograph of one up in his bedroom. A beautiful white one, looking over a gate. His father gave it to him a few years ago, off a calendar he'd printed – and he's never taken it down . . . And when he was seven or eight, I used to have to read him the same book over and over, all *about* a horse.

DYSART Really?

DORA Yes: it was called Prince, and no one could ride him.

Alan calls from his bed, not looking at his mother.

ALAN *(excited, younger voice)* Why not? . . . Why not? . . . Say it! In his voice!

DARA He loved the idea of animals talking.

DYSART Did he?

ALAN *Say it! Say it! . . . Use his voice!*

DORA *('proud' voice)* 'Because I am faithful!'

Alan giggles.

'My name is Prince, and I'm a Prince among horses! Only my young Master can ride me! Anyone else – I'll *throw off!*'

Alan giggles louder.

And then I remember I used to tell him a funny thing about

falling off horses. Did you know that when Christian cavalry first appeared in the New World, the pagans thought horse and rider was one person?

DYSART Really?

ALAN (*sitting up, amazed*) One person?

DORA Actually, they thought it must be a god.

ALAN *A god!*

DORA It was only when one rider fell off, they realized the truth.

DYSART That's fascinating. I never heard that before.... Can you remember anything else like that you may have told him about horses?

DORA Well, not really. They're in the Bible, of course. 'He saith among the trumpets, Ha, ha.'

DYSART Ha, ha?

DORA The Book of Job. Such a noble passage. *You* know – (*quoting*) 'Hast thou given the horse strength?'

ALAN (*responding*) 'Hast thou clothed his neck with thunder?'

DORA (*to Alan*) 'The glory of his nostrils is terrible!'

ALAN 'He swallows the ground with fierceness and rage!'

DORA 'He saith among the trumpets –'

ALAN (*trumpeting*) 'Ha! Ha!'

DORA (*to Dysart*) Isn't that splendid?

DYSART It certainly is.

ALAN (*trumpeting*) Ha! Ha!

DORA And then, of course, we saw an awful lot of Westerns on the television. He couldn't have enough of those.

DYSART But surely you don't have a set, do you? I understood Mr Strang doesn't approve.

DORA (*conspiratorially*) He doesn't ... I used to let him slip off in the afternoons to a friend next door.

DYSART (*smiling*) You mean without his father's knowledge?

DORA What the eye does not see, the heart does not grieve over, does it? Anyway, Westerns are harmless enough, surely?

Frank stands up and enters the square. Alan lies back under the blanket.

15

(*to Frank*) Oh, hallo dear. This is Dr Dysart.

FRANK (*shaking hands*) How d'you do?

DYSART How d'you do?

DORA I was just telling the Doctor, Alan's always adored horses.

FRANK (*tight*) We assumed he did.

DORA You know he did, dear. Look how he liked that photograph you gave him.

FRANK (*startled*) What about it?

DORA Nothing dear. Just that he pestered you to have it as soon as he saw it. Do you remember? (*to Dysart*) We've always been a horsey family. At least my side of it has. My grandfather used to ride every morning on the downs behind Brighton, all dressed up in bowler hat and jodhpurs! He used to look splendid. Indulging in equitation, he called it.

Frank moves away from them and sits wearily.

ALAN (*trying the word*) Equitation....

DORA I remember I told him how that came from *equus*, the Latin word for horse. Alan was fascinated by that word, I know. I suppose because he'd never come across one with two U's together before.

ALAN (*savouring it*) Equus!

DORA I always wanted the boy to ride himself. He'd have so enjoyed it.

DYSART But surely he did?

DORA No.

DYSART Never?

DORA He didn't care for it. He was most definite about not wanting to.

DYSART But he must have had to at the stables? I mean, it would be part of the job.

DORA You'd have thought so, but no. He absolutely wouldn't, would he, dear?

FRANK (*dryly*) It seems he was perfectly happy raking out manure.

DYSART Did he ever give a reason for this?

16

DORA No. I must say we both thought it most peculiar, but he wouldn't discuss it. I mean, you'd have thought he'd be longing to get out in the air after being cooped up all week in that dreadful shop. Electrical and kitchenware! Isn't *that* an environment for a sensitive boy, Doctor?...

FRANK Dear, have you offered the doctor a cup of tea?

DORA Oh dear, no, I haven't!... And you must be dying for one.

DYSART That would be nice.

DORA Of course it would... Excuse me...

She goes out – but lingers on the circle, eavesdropping near the right door. Alan stretches out under his blanket and sleeps. Frank gets up.

FRANK My wife has romantic ideas, if you receive my meaning.

DYSART About her family?

FRANK She thinks she married beneath her. I daresay she did. I don't understand these things myself.

DYSART Mr Strang, I'm fascinated by the fact that Alan wouldn't ride.

FRANK Yes, well that's him. He's always been a weird lad, I have to be honest. Can you imagine spending your weekends like that – just cleaning out stalls – with all the things that he could have been doing in the way of Further Education?

DYSART Except he's hardly a scholar.

FRANK How do we know? He's never really tried. His mother indulged him. She doesn't care if he can hardly write his own name, and she a school teacher that was. Just as long as he's happy, she says...

Dora wrings her hands in anguish. Frank sits again.

DYSART Would you say she was closer to him than you are?

FRANK They've always been thick as thieves. I can't say I entirely approve – especially when I hear her whispering that Bible to him hour after hour, up there in his room.

DYSART Your wife is religious?

FRANK Some might say excessively so. Mind you, that's her business. But when it comes to dosing it down the boy's throat – well, frankly, he's my son as well as hers. She

17

doesn't see that. Of course, that's the funny thing about religious people. They always think their susceptibilities are more important than non-religious.

DYSART And you're non-religious, I take it?

FRANK I'm an atheist, and I don't mind admitting it. If you want my opinion, it's the Bible that's responsible for all this.

DYSART Why?

FRANK Well, look at it yourself. A boy spends night after night having this stuff read into him: an innocent man tortured to death – thorns driven into his head – nails into his hands – a spear jammed through his ribs. It can mark anyone for life, that kind of thing. I'm not joking. The boy was absolutely fascinated by all that. He was always mooning over religious pictures. I mean real kinky ones, if you receive my meaning. I had to put a stop to it once or twice!... (*pause*) Bloody religion – it's our only real problem in this house, but it's insuperable: I don't mind admitting it.

Unable to stand any more, Dora comes in again.

DORA (*pleasantly*) You must excuse my husband, Doctor. This one subject is something of an obsession with him, isn't it, dear? You must admit.

FRANK Call it what you like. All that stuff to me is just bad sex.

DORA And what has that got to do with Alan?

FRANK Everything!... (*seriously*) Everything, Dora!

DORA I don't understand. What are you saying?

He turns away from her.

DYSART (*calmingly*) Mr Strang, exactly how informed do you judge your son to *be* about sex?

FRANK (*tight*) I don't know.

DYSART You didn't actually instruct him yourself?

FRANK Not in so many words, no.

DYSART Did *you*, Mrs Strang?

DORA Well, I spoke a little, yes. I had to. I've been a teacher, Doctor, and I know what happens if you don't. They find out through magazines and dirty books.

DYSART What sort of thing did you tell him? I'm sorry if this is embarrassing.

DORA I told him the biological facts. But I also told him what I believed. That sex is not *just* a biological matter, but spiritual as well. That if God willed, he would fall in love one day. That his task was to prepare himself for the most important happening of his life. And after that, if he was lucky, . he might come to know a higher love still... I simply... don't understand.... *Alan!*...

She breaks down in sobs. Her husband gets up and goes to her.

FRANK (*embarrassed*) There now. There now, Dora. Come on!

DORA (*with sudden desperation*) All right – laugh! Laugh, as usual!

FRANK (*kindly*) No one's laughing, Dora.

She glares at him. He puts his arms round her shoulders.

No one's laughing, are they Doctor?

Tenderly, he leads his wife out of the square, and they resume their places on the bench.

Lights grow much dimmer.

8

A strange noise begins. Alan begins to murmur from his bed. He is having a bad nightmare, moving his hands and body as if frantically straining to tug something back. Dysart leaves the square as the boy's cries increase.

ALAN Ek!... Ek!... *Ek!*...

Cries of Ek! *on tape fill the theatre, from all around. Dysart reaches the foot of Alan's bed as the boy gives a terrible cry —*

EK!

— and wakes up. The sounds snap off. Alan and the Doctor stare at each other. Then abruptly Dysart leaves the area and re-enters the square.

19

9

Lights grow brighter.

Dysart sits on his bench, left, and opens his file. Alan gets out of bed, leaves his blanket, and comes in. He looks truculent.

DYSART Hallo. How are you this morning?

Alan stares at him.

Come on: sit down.

Alan crosses the stage and sits on the bench, opposite.

Sorry if I gave you a start last night. I was collecting some papers from my office, and I thought I'd look in on you. Do you dream often?

ALAN Do *you?*

DYSART It's my job to ask the questions. Yours to answer them.

ALAN Says who?

DYSART Says me. Do you dream often?

ALAN Do you?

DYSART Look – Alan.

ALAN I'll answer if you answer. In turns.

Pause.

DYSART Very well. Only we have to speak the truth.

ALAN (*mocking*) Very well.

DYSART So. Do you dream often?

ALAN Yes. Do you?

DYSART Yes. Do you have a special dream?

ALAN No. Do you?

DYSART Yes. What was your dream about last night?

ALAN Can't remember. What's yours about?

DYSART I said the truth.

ALAN That is the truth. What's yours about? The special one.

DYSART Carving up children.

Alan smiles.

My turn!

ALAN What?

DYSART What is your first memory of a horse?

ALAN What d'you mean?

DYSART The first time one entered your life, in any way.

ALAN Can't remember.

DYSART Are you sure?

ALAN Yes.

DYSART You have no recollection of the first time you noticed
   a horse?

ALAN I told you. Now it's my turn. Are you married?

DYSART (*controlling himself*) I am.

ALAN Is she a doctor too?

DYSART It's my turn.

ALAN Yes, well what?

DYSART What is Ek?

Pause.

   You shouted it out last night in your sleep. I thought you
   might like to talk about it.

ALAN (*singing*) Double Diamond works wonders,

   Works wonders, works wonders!

DYSART Come on, now. You can do better than that.

ALAN (*singing louder*) Double Diamond works wonders,

   Works wonders

   For you!

DYSART All right. Good morning.

ALAN What d'you mean?

DYSART We're finished for today.

ALAN But I've only had ten minutes.

DYSART Too bad.

He picks up a file and studies it. Alan lingers.

   Didn't you hear me? I said, Good morning.

ALAN That's not fair!

DYSART No?

ALAN (*savagely*) The Government pays you twenty quid an
   hour to see me. I know. I heard downstairs.

DYSART Well, go back there and hear some more.

ALAN *That's not fair!*

21

He springs up clenching his fists in a sudden violent rage.

You're a – you're a – You're a swiz!...Bloody swiz!...
Fucking swiz!

DYSART Do I have to call Nurse?

ALAN She puts a finger on me, I'll bash her!

DYSART She'll bash you much harder, I can assure you. Now
go away.

He reads his file. Alan stays where he is, emptily clenching his hands. He turns away.

A pause.

A faint hum starts from the Chorus.

ALAN (*sullenly*) On a beach. . . .

10

He steps out of the square, upstage, and begins to walk round the circle. Warm light glows on it.

DYSART What?

ALAN Where I saw a horse. Swizzy.

Lazily he kicks at the sand, and throws stones at the sea.

DYSART How old were you?

ALAN How should I know? . . . Six.

DYSART Well, go on. What were you doing there?

ALAN Digging.

He throws himself on the ground, downstage centre of the circle, and starts scuffing with his hands.

DYSART A sandcastle?

ALAN Well, what else?

DYSART (*warningly*) And?

ALAN Suddenly I heard this noise. Coming up behind me.

A young Horseman issues in slow motion *out of the tunnel. He carries a riding crop with which he is urging on his invisible horse, down the right side of the circle.*

The hum increases.

DYSART What noise?

ALAN Hooves. Splashing.

DYSART Splashing?

ALAN The tide was out and he was galloping.

DYSART Who was?

ALAN This fellow. Like a college chap. He was on a big horse
– urging him on. I thought he hadn't seen me. I called out:
Hey!

The horseman goes into natural time, *charging fast round the down-stage corner of the square straight at Alan.*

and they just swerved in time!

HORSEMAN (*reining back*) Whoa!...Whoa there! *Whoa!...*
Sorry! I didn't see you!...Did I scare you?

ALAN No!

HORSEMAN (*looking down on him*) That's a terrific castle!

ALAN What's his name?

HORSEMAN Trojan. You can stroke him, if you like. He won't
mind.

Shyly Alan stretches up on tip-toe, and pats an invisible shoulder.

(*amused*) You can hardly reach down there. Would you like
to come up?

Alan nods, eyes wide.

All right. Come round this side. You always mount a horse
from the left. I'll give you a lift. O.K.?

Alan goes round on the other side.

Here we go, now. Just do nothing. Upsadaisy!

*Alan set his foot on the Horseman's thigh, and is lifted by him up on to
his shoulders.*

The hum from the Chorus becomes exultant. Then stops.

All right?

Alan nods.

Good. Now all you do is hold onto his mane.

He holds up the crop, and Alan grips on to it.

Tight now. And grip with your knees. All right?

All set? ... Come on, then, Trojan. Let's go!

The Horseman walks slowly upstage round the circle, with Alan's legs tight round his neck.

DYSART How was it? Was it wonderful?

Alan rides in silence.

   Can't you remember?

HORSEMAN Do you want to go faster?

ALAN Yes!

HORSEMAN O.K. All you have to do is say 'Come on, Trojan –
   bear me away!' . . . Say it, then!

ALAN Bear me away!

The Horesman starts to run with Alan round the circle.

DYSART You went fast?

ALAN Yes!

DYSART Weren't you frightened?

ALAN No!

HORSEMAN Come on now, Trojan! Bear us away! Hold on!
   Come on now! . . .

*He runs faster. Alan begins to laugh. Then suddenly, as they reach again
the right downstage corner, Frank and Dora stand up in alarm.*

DORA Alan!

FRANK Alan!

DORA Alan, stop!

Frank runs round after them. Dora follows behind.

FRANK Hey, you! *You!* . . .

HORSEMAN Whoa, boy! . . . Whoa! . . .

*He reins the horse round, and wheels to face the parents. This all goes
fast.*

FRANK What do you imagine you are doing?

HORSEMAN *(ironic)* 'Imagine'?

FRANK What is my son doing up there?

HORSEMAN Water-skiing!

Dora joins them, breathless.

DORA Is he all right, Frank? . . . He's not hurt?

FRANK Don't you think you should ask permission before
   doing a stupid thing like that?

HORSEMAN What's stupid?

ALAN It's lovely, dad!

DORA Alan, come down here!

HORSEMAN The boy's perfectly safe. Please don't be hysterical.

FRANK Don't you be la-di-da with me, young man! Come down here, Alan. You heard what your mother said.

ALAN No.

FRANK Come down at once. Right this moment.

ALAN No. ... NO!

FRANK (*in a fury*) I said – this moment!

He pulls Alan from the Horseman's shoulders. The boy shrieks, and falls to the ground.

HORSEMAN Watch it!

DORA Frank!

She runs to her son, and kneels. The Horseman skitters.

HORSEMAN Are you mad? D'you want to terrify the horse?

DORA He's grazed his knee. Frank – the boy's hurt!

ALAN I'm not! I'm *not!*

FRANK What's your name?

HORSEMAN Jesse James.

DORA Frank, he's bleeding!

FRANK I intend to report you to the police for endangering the lives of children.

HORSEMAN Go right ahead!

DORA Can you stand, dear?

ALAN Oh, *stop* it! ...

FRANK You're a public menace, d'you know that? How dare you pick up children and put them on dangerous animals.

HORSEMAN Dangerous?

FRANK Of course dangerous. Look at his eyes. They're rolling.

HORSEMAN So are yours!

FRANK In my opinion that is a dangerous animal. In my considered opinion you are both dangers to the safety of this beach.

HORSEMAN And in my opinion, you're a stupid fart!

DORA Frank, leave it!

FRANK What did you say?

DORA It's not important, Frank – really!

25

FRANK *What did you say?*

HORSEMAN Oh bugger off! Sorry, chum! Come on, Trojan!

He urges his horse straight at them, then wheels it and gallops off round the right side of the circle and away up the tunnel, out of sight. The parents cry out, as they are covered with sand and water. Frank runs after him, and round the left side of the circle, with his wife following after.

ALAN Splash, splash, splash! All three of us got covered with water! Dad got absolutely soaked!

FRANK (*shouting after the Horseman*) Hooligan! Filthy hooligan!

ALAN I wanted to laugh!

FRANK Upper class riff-raff! That's all they are, people who go riding! That's what they *want* – trample on ordinary people!

DORA Don't be absurd, Frank.

FRANK It's why they do it. It's why they bloody do it!

DORA (*amused*) Look at you. You're covered!

FRANK Not as much as you. There's sand all over your hair!

She starts to laugh.

(*shouting*) Hooligan! Bloody hooligan!

She starts to laugh more. He tries to brush the sand out of her hair.

What are you laughing at? It's not funny. It's not funny at all, Dora!

She goes off, right, still laughing. Alan edges into the square, still on the ground.

It's just not funny!...

Frank returns to his place on the beach, sulky.

Abrupt silence.

ALAN And that's all I remember.

DYSART And a lot, too. Thank you... You know, I've never been on a horse in my life.

ALAN (*not looking at him*) Nor me.

DYSART You mean, after that?

ALAN Yes.

DYSART But you must have done at the stables?

ALAN No.

DYSART Never?

ALAN No.

DYSART How come?

ALAN I didn't care to.

DYSART Did it have anything to do with falling off like that, all those years ago?

ALAN (*tight*) I just didn't care to, that's all.

DYSART Do you think of that scene often?

ALAN I suppose.

DYSART Why, do you think?

ALAN 'Cos it's funny.

DYSART Is that all?

ALAN What else? My turn. . . . I told you a secret: now you tell me one.

DYSART All right. I have patients who've got things to tell me, only they're ashamed to say them to my face. What do you think I do about that?

ALAN What?

DYSART I give them this little tape recorder.

He takes a small tape recorder and microphone from his pocket.

They go off to another room, and send me the tape through Nurse. They don't have to listen to it with me.

ALAN That's stupid.

DYSART All you do is press this button, and speak into this. It's very simple. Anyway, your time's up for today. I'll see you tomorrow.

ALAN (*getting up*) Maybe.

DYSART Maybe?

ALAN If I feel like it.

He is about to go out. Then suddenly he returns to Dysart and takes the machine from him.

It's stupid.

He leaves the square and goes back to his bed.

11

DORA (*calling out*) Doctor!

Dora re-enters and comes straight on to the square from the right. She wears an overcoat, and is nervously carrying a shopping bag.

DYSART That same evening, his mother appeared.

DORA Hallo, Doctor.

DYSART Mrs Strang!

DORA I've been shopping in the neighbourhood. I thought I might just look in.

DYSART Did you want to see Alan?

DORA (*uncomfortably*) No, no... Not just at the moment. Actually, it's more you I wanted to see.

DYSART Yes?

DORA You see, there's something Mr Strang and I thought you ought to know. We discussed it, and it might just be important.

DYSART Well, come and sit down.

DORA I can't stay more than a moment. I'm late as it is. Mr Strang will be wanting his dinner.

DYSART Ah. (*encouragingly*) So, what was it you wanted to tell me?

She sits on the upstage bench.

DORA Well, do you remember that photograph I mentioned to you. The one Mr Strang gave Alan to decorate his bedroom a few years ago?

DYSART Yes. A horse looking over a gate, wasn't it?

DORA That's right. Well, actually, it took the place of another kind of picture altogether.

DYSART What kind?

DORA It was a reproduction of Our Lord on his way to Calvary. Alan found it in Reeds Art Shop, and fell absolutely in love with it. He insisted on buying it with his pocket money, and hanging it at the foot of his bed where he could see it last thing at night. My husband was very displeased.

DYSART Because it was religious?

DORA In all fairness I must admit it was a little extreme. The Christ was loaded down with chains, and the centurions were really laying on the stripes. It certainly would not have been my choice, but I don't believe in interfering too much with children, so I said nothing.

DYSART But Mr Strang did?

DORA He stood it for a while, but one day we had one of our tiffs about religion, and he went straight upstairs, tore it off the boy's wall and threw it in the dustbin. Alan went quite hysterical. He cried for days without stopping – and he was not a crier, you know.

DYSART But he recovered when he was given the photograph of the horse in its place?

DORA He certainly seemed to. At least, he hung it in exactly the same position, and we had no more of that awful weeping.

DYSART Thank you, Mrs Strang. That *is* interesting ... Exactly how long ago was that? Can you remember?

DORA It must be five years ago, Doctor. Alan would have been about twelve. How is he, by the way?

DYSART Bearing up.

She rises.

DORA Please give him my love.

DYSART You can see him any time you want, you know.

DORA Perhaps if I could come one afternoon without Mr Strang. He and Alan don't exactly get on at the moment, as you can imagine.

DYSART Whatever you decide, Mrs Strang ... Oh, one thing.

DORA Yes?

DYSART Could you describe that photograph of the horse in a little more detail for me? I presume it's still in his bedroom?

DORA Oh, yes. It's a most remarkable picture, really. You very rarely see a horse taken from that angle – absolutely head on. That's what makes it so interesting.

DYSART Why? What does it look like?

DORA Well, it's most extraordinary. It comes out all eyes.

DYSART Staring straight at you?

DORA Yes, that's right . . .

An uncomfortable pause.

I'll come and see him one day very soon, Doctor. Goodbye.

She leaves, and resumes her place by her husband.

DYSART (*to audience*) It was then – that moment – I felt real alarm. What was it? The shadow of a giant head across my desk? . . . At any rate, the feeling got worse with the stable-owner's visit.

12

Dalton comes in to the square: heavy-set: mid-fifties.

DALTON Dr Dysart?

DYSART Mr Dalton. It's very good of you to come.

DALTON It is, actually. In my opinion the boy should be in prison. Not in a hospital at the tax-payers' expense.

DYSART Please sit down.

Dalton sits.

This must have been a terrible experience for you.

DALTON Terrible? I don't think I'll ever get over it. Jill's had a nervous breakdown.

DYSART Jill?

DALTON The girl who worked for me. Of course, she feels responsible in a way. Being the one who introduced him in the first place.

DYSART He was introduced to the stable by a girl?

DALTON Jill Mason. He met her somewhere, and asked for a job. She told him to come and see me. I wish to Christ she never had.

DYSART But when he first appeared he didn't seem in any way peculiar?

DALTON No, he was bloody good. He'd spend hours with the horses cleaning and grooming them, way over the call of duty. I thought he was a real find.

DYSART Apparently, during the whole time he worked for you, he never actually rode.

DALTON That's true.

DYSART Wasn't that peculiar?

DALTON Very ... *If* he didn't.

DYSART What do you mean?

Dalton rises.

DALTON Because on and off, that whole year, I had the feeling the horses were being taken out at night.

DYSART At night?

DALTON There were just odd things I noticed. I mean too often one or other of them would be sweaty first thing in the morning, when it wasn't sick. Very sweaty, too. And its stall wouldn't be near as mucky as it should be if it had been in all night. I never paid it much mind at the time. It was only when I realised I'd been hiring a loony, I came to wonder if he hadn't been riding all the time, behind our backs.

DYSART But wouldn't you have noticed if things had been disturbed?

DALTON Nothing ever was. Still, he's a neat worker. That wouldn't prove anything.

DYSART Aren't the stables locked at night?

DALTON Yes.

DYSART And someone sleeps on the premises?

DALTON Me and my son.

DYSART Two people?

DALTON I'm sorry, Doctor. It's obviously just my fancy. I tell you, this thing has shaken me so bad, I'm liable to believe anything. If there's nothing else, I'll be going.

DYSART Look: even if you were right, why should anyone do that? Why would any boy prefer to ride by himself at night, when he could go off with others during the day.

DALTON Are you asking me? He's a loony, isn't he?

Dalton leaves the square and sits again in his place. Dysart watches him go.

ALAN It was *sexy*.

DYSART His tape arrived that evening.

13

Alan is sitting on his bed holding the tape-recorder. Nurse approaches briskly, takes the machine from him – gives it to Dysart in the square – and leaves again, resuming her seat. Dysart switches on the tape.

ALAN That's what you want to know, isn't it? All right: it was. I'm talking about the beach. That time when I was a kid. What I told you about....

Pause. He is in great emotional difficulty.

Dysart sits on the left bench listening, file in hand. Alan rises and stands directly behind him, but on the circle, as if recording the ensuing speech. He never, of course, looks directly at the Doctor.

I was pushed forward on the horse. There was sweat on my legs from his neck. The fellow held me tight, and let me turn the horse which way I wanted. All that power going any way you wanted ... His sides were all warm, and the smell ... Then suddenly I was on the ground, where Dad pulled me. I could have bashed him ...

Pause.

Something else. When the horse first appeared, I looked up into his mouth. It was huge. There was this chain in it. The fellow pulled it, and cream dripped out. I said 'Does it hurt?' And he said – the horse said – said –

He stops, in anguish. Dysart makes a note in his file.

(*desperately*) It was always the same, after that. Every time I heard one clop by, I had to run and see. Up a country lane or anywhere. They sort of pulled me. I couldn't take my eyes off them. Just to watch their skins. The way their necks twist, and sweat shines in the folds ... (*pause*) I can't remember when it started. Mum reading to me about Prince who no one could ride, except one boy. Or the white horse in

Revelations. 'He that sat upon him was called Faithful and True. His eyes were as flames of fire, and he had a name written that no man knew but himself'... Words like reins. Stirrup. Flanks... 'Dashing his spurs against his charger's flanks!'... Even the words made me feel –... Years, I never told anyone. Mum wouldn't understand. She likes 'Equitation'. Bowler hats and jodhpurs! 'My grandfather dressed for the horse,' she says. What does that mean? The horse isn't dressed. It's the most naked thing you ever saw! More than a dog or a cat or anything. Even the most broken down old nag has got its *life!* To put a bowler on it is *filthy!*... Putting them through their paces! Bloody gymkhanas!... No one understands!... Except cowboys. They do. I wish I was a cowboy. They're free. They just swing up and then it's miles of grass... I bet all cowboys are *orphans!*... I bet they are!

NURSE Mr Strang to see you, Doctor.

DYSART (*in surprise*) Mr Strang? Show him up, please.

ALAN No one ever says to cowboys 'Receive my meaning'! They wouldn't dare. Or 'God' all the time. (*mimicking his mother*) 'God sees you, Alan. God's got eyes everywhere—'

He stops abruptly.

I'm not doing any more!... I hate this!... You can whistle for anymore. I've had it!

He returns angrily to his bed, throwing the blanket over him. Dysart switches off the tape.

14

Frank Strang comes into the square, his hat in his hand. He is nervous and embarrassed.

DYSART (*welcoming*) Hallo, Mr Strang.

FRANK I was just passing. I hope it's not too late.

DYSART Of course not. I'm delighted to see you.

FRANK My wife doesn't know I'm here. I'd be grateful to you if you didn't enlighten her, if you receive my meaning.

DYSART Everything that happens in this room is confidential, Mr Strang.

FRANK I hope so ... I hope so ...

DYSART (*gently*) Do you have something to tell me?

FRANK As a matter of fact I have. Yes.

DYSART Your wife told me about the photograph.

FRANK I know, it's not that! It's *about* that, but it's – worse. ... I wanted to tell you the other night, but I couldn't in front of Dora. Maybe I should have. It might show her where all that stuff leads to, she drills into the boy behind my back.

DYSART What kind of thing is it?

FRANK Something I witnessed.

DYSART Where?

FRANK At home. About eighteen months ago.

DYSART Go on.

FRANK It was late. I'd gone upstairs to fetch sómething. The boy had been in bed hours, or so I thought.

DYSART Go on.

FRANK As I came along the passage I saw the door of his bedroom was ajar. I'm sure he didn't know it was. From inside I heard the sound of this chanting.

DYSART Chanting?

FRANK Like the Bible. One of those lists his mother's always reading to him.

DYSART What kind of list?

FRANK Those Begats. So-and-so begat, you know. Genealogy.

DYSART Can you remember what Alan's list sounded like?

FRANK Well, the *sort* of thing. I stood there absolutely astonished. The first word I heard was ...

ALAN (*rising and chanting*) *Prince!*

DYSART Prince?

FRANK Prince begat Prance. That sort of nonsense.

Alan moves slowly to the centre of the circle, downstage.

ALAN And Prance begat Prankus! And Prankus begat Flankus!

FRANK I looked through the door, and he was standing in the moonlight in his pyjamas, right in front of that big photograph.

DYSART The horse with the huge eyes?

FRANK Right.

ALAN Flankus begat Spankus. And Spankus begat Spunkus the Great, who lived three score years!

FRANK It was all like that. I can't remember the exact names, of course. Then suddenly he knelt down.

DYSART In front of the photograph?

FRANK Yes. Right there at the foot of his bed.

ALAN (*kneeling*) And Legwus begat Neckwus. And Neckwus begat Fleckwus, the King of Spit. And Fleckwus spoke out of his chinkle-chankle!

He bows himself to the ground.

DYSART What?

FRANK I'm sure that was the word. I've never forgotten it. Chinkle-chankle.

Alan raises his head and extends his hands up in glory.

ALAN And he said 'Behold – I give you Equus, my only begotten son!'

DYSART Equus?

FRANK Yes. No doubt of that. He repeated that word several times. 'Equus my only begotten son.'

ALAN (*reverently*) Ek . . . . wus!

DYSART (*suddenly understanding: almost 'aside'*) Ek. . . . Ek. . . .

FRANK (*embarrassed*) And then. . .

DYSART Yes: what?

FRANK He took a piece of string out of his pocket. Made up into a noose. And put it in his mouth.

Alan bridles himself with invisible string, and pulls it back.

And then with his other hand he picked up a coat hanger. A wooden coat hanger, and – and—

DYSART Began to beat himself?

Alan, in mime, begins to thrash himself, increasing the strokes in speed and viciousness.

Pause.

FRANK You see why I couldn't tell his mother.... Religion. Religion's at the bottom of all this!

DYSART What did you do?

FRANK Nothing. I coughed – and went back downstairs.

The boy starts guiltily – tears the string from his mouth – and scrambles back to bed.

DYSART Did you ever speak to him about it later? Even obliquely?

FRANK (*unhappily*) I can't speak of things like that, Doctor. It's not in my nature.

DYSART (*kindly*) No. I see that.

FRANK But I thought you ought to know. So I came.

DYSART (*warmly*) Yes. I'm very grateful to you. Thank you.

Pause.

FRANK Well, that's it ...

DYSART Is there anything else?

FRANK (*even more embarrassed*) There is actually. One thing.

DYSART What's that?

FRANK On the night that he did it – that awful thing in the stable –

DYSART Yes?

FRANK That very night, he was out with a girl.

DYSART How d'you know that?

FRANK I just know.

DYSART (*puzzled*) Did he tell you?

FRANK I can't say any more.

DYSART I don't quite understand.

FRANK Everything said in here is confidential, you said.

DYSART Absolutely.

FRANK Then ask him. Ask him about taking a girl out, that very night he did it.... (*abruptly*) Goodbye, Doctor.

He goes. Dysart looks after him. Frank resumes his seat.

15

Alan gets up and enters the square.

DYSART Alan! Come in. Sit down. (*pleasantly*) What did you do last night?

ALAN Watched telly.

DYSART Any good?

ALAN All right.

DYSART Thanks for the tape. It was excellent.

ALAN I'm not making any more.

DYSART One thing I didn't quite understand. You began to say something about the horse on the beach talking to you.

ALAN That's stupid. Horses don't talk.

DYSART So I believe.

ALAN I don't know what you mean.

DYSART Never mind. Tell me something else. Who introduced you to the stable to begin with?

Pause.

ALAN Someone I met.

DYSART Where?

ALAN Bryson's.

DYSART The shop where you worked?

ALAN Yes.

DYSART That's a funny place for you to be. Whose idea was that?

ALAN Dad.

DYSART I'd thought he'd have wanted you to work with him.

ALAN I haven't the aptitude. And printing's a failing trade. If you receive my meaning.

DYSART (*amused*) I see... What did your mother think?

ALAN Shops are common.

DYSART And you?

ALAN I loved it.

DYSART Really?

ALAN (*sarcastic*) Why not? You get to spend every minute with
  electrical things. It's fun.

Nurse, Dalton and the actors playing horses call out to him as Custom-
ers, seated where they are. Their voices are aggressive and demanding.
There is a constant background mumbling, made up of trade names, out
of which can clearly be distinguished the italicized words, which are
shouted out.

CUSTOMER *Philco!*

ALAN (*to Dysart*) Of course it might just drive you off your
  chump.

CUSTOMER I want to buy a hot-plate. I'm told the *Philco* is a
  good make!

ALAN I think it is, madam.

CUSTOMER *Remington* ladies' shavers?

ALAN I'm not sure, madam.

CUSTOMER *Robex* tableware?

CUSTOMER *Croydex?*

CUSTOMER *Volex?*

CUSTOMER *Pifco* automatic toothbrushes?

ALAN I'll find out, sir.

CUSTOMER *Beautiflor!*

CUSTOMER *Windolene!*

CUSTOMER I want a *Philco* transistor radio!

CUSTOMER This isn't a *Remington!* I wanted a *Remington!*

ALAN Sorry.

CUSTOMER Are you a dealer for *Hoover?*

ALAN Sorry.

CUSTOMER I wanted the heat retaining *Pifco!*

ALAN *Sorry!*

Jill comes into the square: a girl in her early twenties, pretty and middle
class. She wears a sweater and jeans. The mumbling stops.

JILL Hallo.

ALAN Hallo.

JILL Have you any blades for a clipping machine?

ALAN Clipping?

JILL To clip horses.

38

Pause. He stares at her, open-mouthed.

What's the matter?

ALAN You work at Dalton's stables. I've seen you.

During the following, he mimes putting away a pile of boxes on a shelf in the shop.

JILL I've seen you too, haven't I? You're the boy who's always staring into the yard around lunch-time.

ALAN Me?

JILL You're there most days.

ALAN Not me.

JILL (*amused*) Of course it's you. Mr Dalton was only saying the other day: 'Who's that boy keeps staring in at the door?' Are you looking for a job or something?

ALAN (*eagerly*) Is there one?

JILL I don't know.

ALAN I can only do weekends.

JILL That's when most people ride. We can always use extra hands. It'd mainly be mucking out.

ALAN I don't mind.

JILL Can you ride?

ALAN No...No...I don't want to.

She looks at him curiously.

Please.

JILL Come up on Saturday. I'll introduce you to Mr Dalton.

She leaves the square.

DYSART When was this? About a year ago?

ALAN I suppose.

DYSART And she did?

ALAN Yes.

Briskly he moves the three benches to form three stalls in the stable.

16

Rich light falls on the square.
An exultant humming from the Chorus.

Tramping is heard. Three actors playing horses rise from their places. Together they unhook three horse masks from the ladders to left and right, put them on with rigid timing, and walk with swaying horse-motion into the square. Their metal hooves stamp on the wood. Their masks turn and toss high above their heads – as they will do sporadically throughout all horse scenes – making the steel gleam in the light.

For a moment they seem to converge on the boy as he stands in the middle of the stable, but then they swiftly turn and take up positions as if tethered by the head, with their invisible rumps towards him, one by each bench.

Alan is sunk in this glowing world of horses. Lost in wonder, he starts almost involuntarily to kneel on the floor in reverence – but is sharply interrupted by the cheery voice of Dalton, coming into the stable, followed by Jill. The boy straightens up guiltily.

DALTON First thing to learn is drill. Learn it and keep to it. I want this place neat, dry and clean at all times. After you've mucked out, Jill will show you some grooming. What we call strapping a horse.

JILL I think Trooper's got a stone.

DALTON Yes? Let's see.

He crosses to the horse by the left bench, who is balancing one hoof on its tip. He picks up the hoof.

You're right. (*to Alan*) See this? This V here. It's what's called a frog. Sort of shock-absorber. Once you pierce that, it takes ages to heal – so you want to watch for it. You clean it out with this. What we call a hoof-pick.

He takes from his pocket an invisible pick.

Mind how you go with it. It's very sharp. Use it like this.

He quickly takes the stone out.

See?

Alan nods, fascinated.

You'll soon get the hang of it. Jill will look after you. What she doesn't know about stables, isn't worth knowing.

JILL (*pleased*) Oh yes, I'm sure!

DALTON (*handing Alan the pick*) Careful how you go with that.

The main rule is, anything you don't know: ask. Never pretend you know something when you don't. (*smiling*) Actually, the main rule is: enjoy yourself. All right?

ALAN Yes, sir.

DALTON Good lad. See you later.

He nods to them cheerfully, and leaves the square. Alan clearly puts the invisible hoof-pick on the rail, downstage left.

JILL All right, let's start on some grooming. Why don't we begin with him? He looks as if he needs it.

They approach Nugget, who is standing to the right. She pats him. Alan sits and watches her.

This is Nugget. He's my favourite. He's as gentle as a baby, aren't you? But terribly fast if you want him to be.

During the following, she mimes both the actions and the objects, which she picks up from the right bench.

Now this is the dandy, and we start with that. Then you move on to the body brush. This is the most important, and you use it with this curry-comb. Now you always groom the same way: from the ears downward. Don't be afraid to do it hard. The harder you do it, the more the horse loves it. Push it right through the coat: like this.

The boy watches in fascination as she brushes the invisible body of Nugget, scraping the dirt and hair off on to the invisible curry-comb. Now and then the horse mask moves very slightly in pleasure.

Down towards the tail and right through the coat. See how he loves it? I'm giving you a lovely massage, boy, aren't I? . . . You try.

She hands him the brush. Gingerly he rises and approaches Nugget. Embarrassed and excited, he copies her movements, inexpertly.

Keep it nice and easy. Never rush. Down towards the tail and right through the coat. That's it. Again. Down towards the tail and right through the coat. . . . Very good. Now you keep that up for fifteen minutes and then do old Trooper. Will you?

Alan nods.

You've got a feel for it. I can tell. It's going to be nice

41

teaching you. See you later.

She leaves the square and resumes her place. Alan is left alone with the horses.

They all stamp. He approaches Nugget again, and touches the horse's shoulder. The mask turns sharply in his direction. The boy pauses, then moves his hand gently over the outline of the neck and back. The mask is re-assured. It stares ahead unmoving. Then Alan lifts his palm to his face and smells it deeply, closing his eyes.

Dysart rises from his bench, and begins to walk slowly upstage round the circle.

DYSART Was that good? Touching them.

Alan gives a faint groan.

ALAN Mmm.

DYSART It must have been marvellous, being near them at last ... Stroking them ... Making them fresh and glossy ... Tell me ...

Silence. Alan begins to brush Nugget.

How about the girl? Did you like her?

ALAN (*tight*) All right.

DYSART Just all right?

Alan changes his position, moving round Nugget's rump so that his back is to the audience. He brushes harder. Dysart comes downstage around the circle, and finally back to his bench.

Was she friendly?

ALAN Yes.

DYSART Or stand-offish?

ALAN Yes.

DYSART Well which?

ALAN What?

DYSART Which was she?

Alan brushes harder.

Did you take her out? Come on now: tell me. Did you have a date with her?

ALAN What?

DYSART (*sitting*) Tell me if you did.

The boy suddenly explodes in one of his rages.

ALAN (*yelling*) TELL ME!
All the masks toss at the noise.
DYSART What?
ALAN *Tell me, tell me, tell me, tell me!*
Alan storms out of the square, and downstage to where Dysart sits. He is raging. During the ensuing, the horses leave by all three openings.

On and on, sitting there! Nosey Parker! That's all you are! Bloody Nosey Parker! Just like Dad. On and on and bloody on! Tell me, tell me, tell me! ... Answer this. Answer that. Never stop! –

He marches round the circle and back into the square. Dysart rises and enters it from the other side.

17

Lights brighten.

DYSART I'm sorry.
Alan slams about what is now the office again, replacing the benches to their usual position.
ALAN All right, it's my turn now. You tell me! Answer me!
DYSART We're not playing that game now.
ALAN We're playing what I say.
DYSART All right. What do you want to know?
He sits.
ALAN Do *you* have dates?
DYSART I told you. I'm married.
Alan approaches him, very hostile.
ALAN I know. Her name's Margaret. She's a dentist! You see, I found out! What made you go with her? Did you use to bite her hands when she did you in the chair?
The boy sits next to him, close.
DYSART That's not very funny.
ALAN Do you have girls behind her back?
DYSART No.

43

ALAN Then what? Do you fuck her?

DYSART That's enough now.

He rises and moves away.

ALAN Come on, tell me! Tell me, tell me!

DYSART I said that's enough now.

Alan rises too and walks around him.

ALAN I bet you don't. I bet you never touch her. Come on, tell me. You've got no kids, have you? Is that because you don't fuck?

DYSART (*sharp*) Go to your room. Go on: quick march.

Pause. Alan moves away from him, insolently takes up a packet of Dysart's cigarettes from the bench, and extracts one.

Give me those cigarettes.

The boy puts one in his mouth.

(*exploding*) Alan, *give them to me!*

Reluctantly Alan shoves the cigarette back in the packet, turns and hands it to him.

Now go!

Alan bolts out of the square, and back to his bed. Dysart, unnerved, addresses the audience.

Brilliant! Absolutely brilliant! The boy's on the run, so he gets defensive. What am *I*, then?... Wicked little bastard – he knew exactly what questions to try. He'd actually marched himself round the hospital, making enquiries about my wife. Wicked and – of course, perceptive. Ever since I made that crack about carving up children, he's been aware of me in an absolutely specific way. Of course, there's nothing novel in that. Advanced neurotics can be dazzling at that game. They aim unswervingly at your area of maximum vulnerability... Which I suppose is as good a way as any of describing Margaret.

He sits. Hesther enters the square.

Light grows warmer.

18

HESTHER Now stop it.

DYSART Do I embarrass you?

HESTHER I suspect you're about to.

Pause.

DYSART My wife doesn't understand me, Your Honour.

HESTHER Do you understand her?

DYSART No. Obviously I never did.

HESTHER I'm sorry. I've never liked to ask but I've always imagined you weren't exactly compatible.

She moves to sit opposite.

DYSART We were. It actually worked for a bit. I mean for both of us. We worked for each other. She actually for me through a kind of briskness. A clear, red-headed, inaccessible briskness which kept me keyed up for months. Mind you, if you're kinky for Northern Hygienic, as I am, you can't find anything much more compelling than a Scottish Lady Dentist.

HESTHER It's *you* who are wicked, you know!

DYSART Not at all: She got exactly the same from me. Antiseptic proficiency. I was like that in those days. We suited each other admirably. I see us in our wedding photo: Doctor and Doctor Mac Brisk. We were brisk in our wooing, brisk in our wedding, brisk in our disappointment. We turned from each other briskly into our separate surgeries: and now there's damn all.

HESTHER You have no children, have you?

DYSART No, we didn't go in for them. Instead, she sits beside our salmon-pink, glazed brick fireplace, and knits things for orphans in a home she helps with. And I sit opposite, turning the pages of art books on Ancient Greece. Occasionally, I still trail a faint scent of my enthusiasm across her path. I pass her a picture of the sacred acrobats of Crete leaping through the horns of running bulls – and she'll say: 'Och, Martin, what an *absurred* thing to be doing! The Highland

Games, now there's *norrmal* sport!' Or she'll observe, just after I've told her a story from the Iliad: 'You know, when you come to think of it, Agamemnon and that lot were nothing but a bunch of ruffians from the Gorbals, only with fancy names!' (*He rises*) You get the picture. She's turned into a Shrink. The familiar domestic monster. Margaret Dysart: the Shrink's Shrink.

HESTHER That's cruel, Martin.

DYSART Yes. Do you know what it's like for two people to live in the same house as if they were in different parts of the world? Mentally, she's always in some drizzly kirk of her own inheriting: and I'm in some Doric temple – clouds tearing through pillars – eagles bearing prophecies out of the sky. She finds all that repulsive. All my wife has ever taken from the Mediterranean – from that whole vast intuitive culture – are four bottles of Chianti to make into lamps, and two china condiment donkeys labelled Sally and Peppy.

Pause.

(*more intimately*) I wish there was one person in my life I could show. One instinctive, absolutely unbrisk person I could take to Greece, and stand in front of certain shrines and sacred streams and say 'Look! Life is only comprehensible through a thousand local Gods. And not just the old dead ones with names like Zeus – no, but living Geniuses of Place and Person! And not just Greece but modern England! Spirits of certain trees, certain curves of brick wall, certain chip shops, if you like, and slate roofs – just as of certain frowns in people and slouches . . . I'd say to them – 'Worship as many as you can see – and more will appear!' . . . If I had a son, I bet you he'd come out exactly like his mother. Utterly worshipless. Would you like a drink?

HESTHER No, thanks. Actually, I've got to be going. As usual . . .

DYSART Really?

HESTHER Really. I've got an Everest of papers to get through before bed.

DYSART You never stop, do you?

HESTHER Do you?

DYSART This boy, with his stare. He's trying to save himself through me.

HESTHER I'd say so.

DYSART What am I trying to do to him?

HESTHER Restore him, surely?

DYSART To what?

HESTHER A normal life.

DYSART Normal?

HESTHER It still means something.

DYSART Does it?

HESTHER Of course.

DYSART You mean a normal boy has one head: a normal head has two ears?

HEATHER You know I don't.

DYSART Then what else?

HESTHER (*lightly*) Oh, stop it.

DYSART No, what? You tell me.

HESTHER (*rising: smiling*) I won't be put on the stand like this, Martin. You're really disgraceful!...(*Pause*) You know what I mean by a normal smile in a child's eyes, and one that isn't – even if I can't exactly define it. Don't you?

DYSART Yes.

HESTHER Then we have a duty to that, surely? Both of us.

DYSART Touché.... I'll talk to you.

HESTHER Dismissed?

DYSART You said you had to go.

HESTHER I do...(*she kisses his cheek*). Thank you for what you're doing.... You're going through a rotten patch at the moment. I'm sorry...I suppose one of the few things one can do is simply hold on to priorities.

DYSART Like what?

HESTHER Oh – children before grown-ups. Things like that.

He contemplates her.

DYSART You're really quite splendid.

47

HESTHER Famous for it. Goodnight.
She leaves him.
DYSART (*to himself – or to the audience*) Normal!...Normal!

19

Alan rises and enters the square. He is subdued.

DYSART Good afternoon.
ALAN Afternoon.
DYSART I'm sorry about our row yesterday.
ALAN It was stupid.
DYSART It was.
ALAN What I said, I mean.
DYSART How are you sleeping?
Alan shrugs.
  You're not feeling well, are you?
ALAN All right.
DYSART Would you like to play a game? It could make you feel
  better.
ALAN What kind?
DYSART It's called *Blink*. You have to fix your eyes on some-
  thing: say, that little stain over there on the wall – and I tap
  this pen on the desk. The first time I tap it, you close your
  eyes. The next time you open them. And so on. Close, open,
  close, open, till I say Stop.
ALAN How can that make you feel better?
DYSART It relaxes you. You'll feel as though you're talking to
  me in your sleep.
ALAN It's stupid.
DYSART You don't have to do it, if you don't want to.
ALAN I didn't say I didn't want to.
DYSART Well?
ALAN I don't mind.
DYSART Good. Sit down and start watching that stain. Put

your hands by your sides, and open the fingers wide.

He opens the left bench and Alan sits on the end of it.

The thing is to feel comfortable, and relax absolutely ... Are you looking at the stain?

ALAN Yes.

DYSART Right. Now try and keep your mind as blank as possible.

ALAN That's not difficult.

DYSART Ssh. Stop talking ... On the first tap, close. On the second, open. Are you ready?

Alan nods. Dysart taps his pen on the wooden rail. Alan shuts his eyes. Dysart taps again. Alan opens them. The taps are evenly spaced. After four of them the sound cuts out, and is replaced by a louder, metallic sound, on tape. Dysart talks through this, to the audience – the light changes to cold – while the boy sits in front of him, staring at the wall, opening and shutting his eyes.

The Normal is the good smile in a child's eyes – all right. It is also the dead stare in a million adults. It both sustains and kills – like a God. It is the Ordinary made beautiful: it is also the Average made lethal. The Normal is the indispensable, murderous God of Health, and I am his Priest. My tools are very delicate. My compassion is honest. I have honestly assisted children in this room. I have talked away terrors and relieved many agonies. But also – beyond question – I have cut from them parts of individuality repugnant to this God, in both his aspects. Parts sacred to rarer and more wonderful Gods. And at what length ... sacrifices to Zeus took at the most, surely, sixty seconds each. Sacrifices to the Normal can take as long as sixty months.

The natural sound of the pencil resumes.

Light changes back.

(*to Alan*) Now your eyes are feeling heavy. You want to sleep, don't you? You want a long, deep sleep. Have it. Your head is heavy. Very heavy. Your shoulders are heavy. Sleep.

The pencil stops. Alan's eyes remain shut and his head has sunk on his chest.

49

Can you hear me?

ALAN Mmm.

DYSART You can speak normally. Say Yes, if you can.

ALAN Yes.

DYSART Good boy. Now raise your head, and open your eyes.

He does so.

Now, Alan, you're going to answer questions I'm going to ask you. Do you understand?

ALAN Yes.

DYSART And when you wake up, you are going to remember everything you tell me. All right?

ALAN Yes.

DYSART Good. Now I want you to think back in time. You are on that beach you told me about. The tide has gone out, and you're making sandcastles. Above you, staring down at you, is that great horse's head, and the cream dropping from it. Can you see that?

ALAN Yes.

DYSART You ask him a question. 'Does the chain hurt?'

ALAN Yes.

DYSART Do you ask him aloud?

ALAN No.

DYSART And what does the horse say back?

ALAN 'Yes.'

DYSART Then what do you say?

ALAN 'I'll take it out for you.'

DYSART And he says?

ALAN 'It never comes out. They have me in chains.'

DYSART Like Jesus?

ALAN Yes!

DYSART Only his name isn't Jesus, is it?

ALAN No.

DYSART What is it?

ALAN No one knows but him and me.

DYSART You can tell me, Alan. Name him.

ALAN Equus.

DYSART Thank you. Does he live in all horses or just some?

ALAN All.

DYSART Good boy. Now: you leave the beach. You're in your bedroom at home. You're twelve years old. You're in front of the picture. You're looking at Equus from the foot of your bed. Would you like to kneel down?

ALAN Yes.

DYSART (*encouragingly*) Go on, then.

Alan kneels.

Now tell me. Why is Equus in chains?

ALAN For the sins of the world.

DYSART What does he say to you?

ALAN 'I see you.' 'I will save you.'

DYSART How?

ALAN 'Bear you away. Two shall be one.'

DYSART Horse and rider shall be one beast?

ALAN One person!

DYSART Go on.

ALAN 'And my chinkle-chankle shall be in thy hand.'

DYSART Chinkle-chankle? That's his mouth chain?

ALAN Yes.

DYSART Good. You can get up...Come on.

Alan rises.

Now: think of the stable. What is the stable? His Temple? His Holy of Holies?

ALAN Yes.

DYSART Where you wash him? Where you tend him, and brush him with many brushes?

ALAN Yes.

DYSART And there he spoke to you, didn't he? He looked at you with his gentle eyes, and spake unto you?

ALAN Yes.

DYSART What did he say? 'Ride me?' 'Mount me, and ride me forth at night'?

ALAN Yes.

DYSART And you obeyed?

ALAN Yes.

DYSART How did you learn? By watching others?

ALAN Yes.

DYSART It must have been difficult. You bounced about?

ALAN Yes.

DYSART But he showed you, didn't he? Equus showed you the way.

ALAN No!

DYSART He didn't?

ALAN He showed me nothing! He's a mean bugger! Ride – or fall! That's Straw Law.

DYSART Straw Law?

ALAN He was born in the straw, and this is his law.

DYSART But you managed? You mastered him?

ALAN Had to!

DYSART And then you rode in secret?

ALAN Yes.

DYSART How often?

ALAN Every three weeks. More, people would notice.

DYSART On a particular horse?

ALAN No.

DYSART How did you get into the stable?

ALAN Stole a key. Had it copied at Bryson's.

DYSART Clever boy.

Alan smiles.

Then you'd slip out of the house?

ALAN Midnight! On the stroke!

DYSART How far's the stable?

ALAN Two miles.

Pause.

DYSART Let's do it! Let's go riding! . . . Now!

He stands up, and pushes in his bench.

You are there now, in front of the stable door.

Alan turns upstage.

That key's in your hand. Go and open it.

20

Alan moves upstage, and mimes opening the door.

Soft light on the circle.

Humming from the Chorus: the Equus Noise.

The horse actors enter, raise high their masks, and put them on all together. They stand around the circle – Nugget in the mouth of the tunnel.

DYSART Quietly as possible. Dalton may still be awake. Sssh . . . Quietly . . . Good. Now go in.

Alan steps secretly out of the square through the central opening on to the circle, now glowing with a warm light. He looks about him. The horses stamp uneasily: their masks turn towards him.

You are on the inside now. All the horses are staring at you. Can you see them?

ALAN (*excited*) Yes!

DYSART Which one are you going to take?

ALAN Nugget.

Alan reaches up and mimes leading Nugget carefully round the circle downstage with a rope, past all the horses on the right.

DYSART What colour is Nugget?

ALAN Chestnut.

The horse picks his way with care. Alan halts him at the corner of the square.

DYSART What do you do, first thing?

ALAN Put on his sandals.

DYSART Sandals?

He kneels, downstage centre.

ALAN Sandals of majesty! . . . Made of sack.

He picks up the invisible sandals, and kisses them devoutly.

Tie them round his hooves.

He taps Nugget's right leg: the horse raises it and the boy mimes tying the sack round it.

DYSART All four hooves?

ALAN Yes.

DYSART Then?

ALAN Chinkle-chankle.

He mimes picking up the bridle and bit.

He doesn't like it so late, but he takes it for my sake. He bends for me. He stretches forth his neck to it.

Nugget bends his head down. Alan first ritually puts the bit into his own mouth, then crosses, and transfers it into Nugget's. He reaches up and buckles on the bridle. Then he leads him by the invisible reins, across the front of the stage and up round the left side of the circle. Nugget follows obediently.

ALAN Buckle and lead out.

DYSART No saddle?

ALAN Never.

DYSART Go on.

ALAN Walk down the path behind. He's quiet. Always is, this bit. Meek and mild legs. At least till the field. Then there's trouble.

The horse jerks back. The mask tosses.

DYSART What kind?

ALAN Won't go in.

DYSART Why not?

ALAN It's his place of Ha Ha.

DYSART What?

ALAN Ha Ha.

DYSART Make him go into it.

ALAN (*whispering fiercely*) Come on!...Come on!...

He drags the horse into the square as Dysart steps out of it.

21

Nugget comes to a halt staring diagonally down what is now the field. The Equus noise dies away. The boy looks about him.

DYSART (*from the circle*) Is it a big field?

ALAN Huge!

DYSART What's it·like?

ALAN Full of mist. Nettles on your feet.

He mimes taking off his shoes – and the sting.

Ah!

DYSART (*going back to his bench*) You take your shoes off?

ALAN Everything.

DYSART All your clothes?

ALAN Yes.

He mimes undressing completely in front of the horse. When he is finished, and obviously quite naked, he throws out his arms and shows himself fully to his God, bowing his head before Nugget.

DYSART Where do you leave them?

ALAN Tree hole near the gate. No one could find them.

He walks upstage and crouches by the bench, stuffing the invisible clothes beneath it. Dysart sits again on the left bench, downstage beyond the circle.

DYSART How does it feel now?

ALAN (*holds himself*) Burns.

DYSART Burns?

ALAN The mist!

DYSART Go on. Now what?

ALAN The Manbit.

He reaches again under the bench and draws out an invisible stick.

DYSART Manbit?

ALAN The stick for my mouth.

DYSART Your mouth?

ALAN To bite on.

DYSART Why? What for?

ALAN So's it won't happen too quick.

DYSART Is it always the same stick?

ALAN Course. Sacred stick. Keep it in the hole. The Ark of the Manbit.

DYSART And now what?... What do you do now?

Pause. He rises and approaches Nugget.

ALAN Touch him!

DYSART Where?

55

ALAN (*in wonder*) All over. Everywhere. Belly. Ribs. His ribs are of ivory. Of great value! . . . His flank is cool. His nostrils open for me. His eyes shine. They can see in the dark . . . *Eyes!*—

Suddenly he dashes in distress to the farthest corner of the square.

DYSART *Go on!* . . . Then?

Pause.

ALAN Give sugar.

DYSART A lump of sugar?

Alan returns to Nugget.

ALAN His Last Supper.

DYSART Last before what?

ALAN Ha Ha.

He kneels before the horse, palms upward and joined together.

DYSART Do you say anything when you give it to him?

ALAN (*offering it*) Take my sins. Eat them for my sake . . . He always does.

Nugget bows the mask into Alan's palm, then takes a step back to eat.
      And then he's ready?

DYSART You can get up on him now?

ALAN Yes!

DYSART Do it, then. Mount him.

Alan, lying before Nugget, stretches out on the square. He grasps the top of the thin metal pole embedded in the wood. He whispers his God's name ceremonially.

ALAN Equus! . . . Equus! . . . Equus!

He pulls the pole upright. The actor playing Nugget leans forward and grabs it. At the same instant all the other horses lean forward around the circle, each placing a gloved hand on the rail. Alan rises and walks right back to the upstage corner, left.

   Take me!

   He runs and jumps high on to Nugget's back.

   (*crying out*) *Ah!*

DYSART What is it?

ALAN Hurts!

DYSART Hurts?

ALAN Knives in his skin! Little knives – all inside my legs.

Nugget mimes restiveness.

ALAN Stay, Equus. No one said Go!... That's it. He's good. Equus the Godslave, Faithful and True. Into my hands he commends himself – naked in his chinkle-chankle. (*he punches Nugget*) Stop it!... He wants to go so badly.

DYSART Go, then. Leave me behind. Ride away now, Alan. Now!... Now you are alone with Equus.

Alan stiffens his body.

ALAN (*ritually*) Equus – son of Fleckwus – son of Neckwus – *Walk.*

A hum from the Chorus.

Very slowly the horses standing on the circle begin to turn the square by gently pushing the wooden rail. Alan and his mount start to revolve. The effect, immediately, is of a statue being slowly turned round on a plinth. During the ride however the speed increases, and the light decreases until it is only a fierce spotlight on horse and rider, with the overspill glinting on the other masks leaning in towards them.

Here we go. The King rides out on Equus, mightiest of horses. Only I can ride him. He lets me turn him this way and that. His neck comes out of my body. It lifts in the dark. Equus, my Godslave!... Now the King commands you. Tonight, we ride against them all.

DYSART Who's all?

ALAN My foes and His.

DYSART Who are your foes?

ALAN The Hosts of Hoover. The Hosts of Philco. The Hosts of Pifco. The House of Remington and all its tribe!

DYSART Who are His foes?

ALAN The Hosts of Jodhpur. The Hosts of Bowler and Gymkhana. All those who show him off for their vanity. Tie rosettes on his head for their vanity! Come on, Equus. Let's get them!... *Trot!*

The speed of the turning square increases.

Stead-y! Stead-y! Stead-y! Stead-y! Cowboys are watching! Take off their stetsons. They know who we are. They're admiring

57

us! Bowing low unto us! Come on now – show them! *Canter!*
. . . CANTER!

He whips Nugget.

And Equus the Mighty rose against All!

His enemies scatter, his enemies fall!

TURN!

Trample them, trample them,

Trample them, trample them,

TURN!

TURN!!

TURN!!!

The Equus noise increases in volume.

(*shouting*) WEE! . . . WAA! . . . WONDERFUL! . . .

I'm stiff! Stiff in the wind!

My mane, stiff in the wind!

My flanks! *My* hooves!

Mane on my legs, on my flanks, like whips!

Raw!

Raw!

I'm raw! Raw!

Feel me on you! *On* you! *On* you! *On* you!

I want to be *in* you!

I want to BE you forever and ever!–

Equus, I love you!

Now! –

Bear me away!

Make us One Person!

He rides Equus frantically.

One Person! One Person! One Person! One Person!

He rises up on the horse's back, and calls like a trumpet.

Ha-HA! . . . Ha-HA! . . . Ha-HA!

The trumpet turns to great cries.

HA-HA! HA-HA! HA-HA! HA-HA! HA! . . . HA! . . . HAAAAA!

He twists like a flame.

Silence.

The turning square comes to a stop in the same position it occupied at the opening of the Act.

   Slowly the boy drops off the horse's back on to the ground. He lowers his head and kisses Nugget's hoof. Finally he flings back his head and cries up to him:

   AMEN!

Nugget snorts, once.

Blackout

Act Two

22

Darkness.

Lights come slowly up on Alan kneeling in the night at the hooves of Nugget. Slowly he gets up, climbing lovingly up the body of the horse until he can stand and kiss it.

Dysart sits on the downstage bench where he began Act One.

DYSART With one particular horse, called Nugget, he embraces. He showed me how he stands with it afterwards in the night, one hand on its chest, one on its neck, like a frozen tango dancer, inhaling its cold sweet breath. 'Have you noticed,' he said, 'about horses: how they'll stand one hoof on its end, like those girls in the ballet?'

Alan leads Nugget out of the square. Dysart rises. The horse walks away up the tunnel and disappears. The boy comes downstage and sits on the bench Dysart has vacated. Dysart crosses downstage and moves slowly up round the circle, until he reaches the central entrance to the square.

Now he's gone off to rest, leaving me alone with Equus. I can hear the creature's voice. It's calling me out of the black cave of the Psyche. I shove in my dim little torch, and there he stands – waiting for me. He raises his matted head. He opens his great square teeth, and says – (*mocking*) '*Why?* ... Why Me? ... Why – ultimately – Me? ... Do you really imagine you can account for Me? Totally, infallibly, inevitably account for Me? ... Poor Doctor Dysart!'

He enters the square.

Of course I've stared at such images before. Or been stared at by them, whichever way you look at it. And weirdly often now with me the feeling is that *they* are staring at *us* – that in some quite palpable way they precede us. Meaningless, but unsettling ... In either case, this one is the most alarming yet. It asks questions I've avoided all my professional life.

(*Pause*) A child is born into a world of phenomena all equal in their power to enslave. It sniffs – it sucks – it strokes its eyes over the whole uncomfortable range. Suddenly one strikes. Why? Moments snap together like magnets, forging a chain of shackles. Why? I can trace them. I can even, with time, pull them apart again. But why at the start they were ever magnetized at all – just those particular moments of experience and no others – I don't know. *And nor does anyone else.* Yet *if* I don't know – if I can never know that – then what am I doing here? I don't mean clinically doing or socially doing – I mean *fundamentally!* These questions, these Whys, are fundamental – yet they have no place in a consulting room. So then, do I?.. This is the feeling more and more with me – No Place. Displacement.... 'Account for me,' says staring Equus. 'First account for Me!...' I fancy this is more than menopause.

Nurse rushes in.

NURSE Doctor!...Doctor! There's a terrible scene with the Strang boy. His mother came to visit him, and I gave her the tray to take in. He threw it at her. She's saying the most dreadful things.

Alan springs up, down left. Dora springs up, down right. They face each other across the bottom end of the stage. It is observable that at the start of this Act Frank is not sitting beside his wife on their bench. It is hopefully not observable that he is placed among the audience upstage, in the gloom, by the central tunnel.

DORA Don't you dare! *Don't you dare!*

DYSART Is she still there?

NURSE Yes!

He quickly leaves the square, followed by the Nurse. Dora moves towards her son.

DORA Don't you look at me like that! I'm not a doctor, you know, who'll take anything. Don't you dare give me that stare, young man!

She slaps his face. Dysart joins them.

DYSART Mrs Strang!

DORA I know your stares. They don't work on me!

DYSART (*to her*) Leave this room.

DORA What did you say?

DYSART I tell you to leave here at once.

Dora hesitates. Then:

DORA Goodbye, Alan.

She walks past her son, and round into the square. Dysart follows her. Both are very upset. Alan returns to his bench and Nurse to her place.

23

Lights up on the square.

DYSART I must ask you never to come here again.

DORA Do you think I want to? Do you think I want to?

DYSART Mrs Strang, what on earth has got into you? Can't you see the boy is highly distressed?

DORA (*ironic*) Really?

DYSART Of course! He's at a most delicate stage of treatment. He's totally exposed. Ashamed. Everything you can imagine!

DORA (*exploding*) And me? What about me? . . . What do you think I am? . . . I'm a parent, of course – so it doesn't count. That's a dirty word in here, isn't it, 'parent'?

DYSART You know that's not true.

DORA Oh, I know. I know, all right! I've heard it all my life. It's *our* fault. Whatever happens, *we* did it. Alan's just a little victim. He's really done nothing at all! (*savagely*) What do you have to do in this world to get any sympathy – blind animals?

DYSART Sit down, Mrs Strang.

DORA (*ignoring him: more and more urgently*) Look, Doctor: you don't have to live with this. Alan is one patient to you: one out of many. He's my son. I lie awake every night thinking about it. Frank lies there beside me. I can hear him. Neither of us sleeps all night. You come to us and say Who forbids television? who does what behind whose back? – as if we're criminals. Let me tell you something. We're not criminals. We've done nothing wrong. We loved Alan. We gave him the best love we could. All right, we quarrel sometimes – all parents quarrel – we always make it up. My husband is a good man. He's an upright man, religion or no religion. He cares for his home, for the world, and for his boy. Alan had love and care and treats, and as much fun as any boy in the world. I know about loveless homes: I was a teacher. Our home wasn't loveless. I know about privacy too – not invading a child's privacy. All right, Frank may be at fault there – he digs into him too much – but nothing in excess. He's not a bully . . . (*gravely*) No, doctor. Whatever's happened has happened *because of Alan*. Alan is himself. Every soul is itself. If you added up everything we ever did to him, from his first day on earth to this, you wouldn't find why he did this terrible thing – because that's *him*: not just all of our things added up. Do you understand what I'm saying? I want you to understand, because I lie awake and awake thinking it out, and I want you to know that I deny it absolutely what he's doing now, staring at me, attacking me for what *he's* done, for what *he* is! (*pause: calmer*) You've got your words, and I've got mine. You call it a complex, I suppose. But if you knew God, Doctor, you would know about the Devil. You'd know the Devil isn't made by what mummy says and daddy says. The Devil's *there*. It's an old-fashioned word, but a true thing . . . I'll go. What I did in there was inexcusable. I only know he was my little Alan, and then the Devil came.

She leaves the square, and resumes her place. Dysart watches her go, then leaves himself by the opposite entrance, and approaches Alan.

24

Seated on his bench, the boy glares at him.

DYSART I thought you liked your mother.
Silence.

She doesn't know anything, you know. I haven't told her what you told me. You do know that, don't you?

ALAN It was lies anyway.

DYSART What?

ALAN You and your pencil. Just a con trick, that's all.

DYSART What do you mean?

ALAN Made me say a lot of lies.

DYSART Did it? . . . Like what?

ALAN All of it. Everything I said. Lot of lies.

Pause.

DYSART I see.

ALAN You ought to be locked up. Your bloody tricks.

DYSART I thought you liked tricks.

ALAN It'll be the drug next. I know.

Dysart turns, sharply.

DYSART What drug?

ALAN I've heard. I'm not ignorant. I know what you get up to in here. Shove needles in people, pump them full of truth drug, so they can't help saying things. That's next, isn't it?

Pause.

DYSART Alan, do you know why you're here?

ALAN So you can give me truth drugs.

He glares at him. Dysart leaves abruptly, and returns to the square.

25

Hesther comes in simultaneously from the other side.

DYSART (*agitated*) He actually thinks they exist! And of course he wants one.

HESTHER It doesn't sound like that to me.

DYSART Of course he does. Why mention them otherwise? He wants a way to speak. To finally tell me what happened in that stable. Tape's too isolated, and hypnosis is a trick. At least that's the pretence.

HESTHER Does he still say that today?

DYSART I haven't seen him. I cancelled his appointment this morning, and let him stew in his own anxiety. Now I am almost tempted to play a real trick on him.

HESTHER (*sitting*) Like what?

DYSART The old placebo.

HESTHER You mean a harmless pill?

DYSART Full of *alleged* Truth Drug. Probably an aspirin.

HESTHER But he'd deny it afterwards. Same thing all over.

DYSART No. Because he's ready to abreact.

HESTHER Abreact?

DYSART Live it all again. He won't be able to deny it after that, because he'll have shown me. Not just told me – but acted it out in front of me.

HESTHER Can you get him to do that?

DYSART I think so. He's nearly done it already. Under all that glowering, he trusts me. Do you realise that?

HESTHER (*warmly*) I'm sure he does.

DYSART Poor bloody fool.

HESTHER Don't start that again.

Pause.

DYSART (*quietly*) Can you think of anything worse one can do to anybody than take away their worship?

HESTHER Worship?

DYSART Yes, that word again!

HESTHER Aren't you being a little extreme?

DYSART Extremity's the point.

HESTHER Worship isn't destructive, Martin. I know that.

DYSART I don't. I only know it's the core of his life. What else has he got? Think about him. He can hardly read. He knows no physics or engineering to make the world real for him. No paintings to show him how others have enjoyed it. No music except television jingles. No history except tales from a desperate mother. No friends. Not one kid to give him a joke, or make him know himself more moderately. He's a modern citizen for whom society doesn't exist. He lives *one hour* every three weeks – howling in a mist. And after the service kneels to a slave who stands over him obviously and unthrowably his master. With my body I thee worship! ... Many men have less vital relationships with their wives.

Pause.

HESTHER All the same, they don't usually blind their wives, do they?

DYSART Oh, come on!

HESTHER Well, do they?

DYSART (*sarcastically*) You mean he's dangerous? A violent, dangerous madman who's going to run round the country doing it again and again?

HESTHER I mean he's in pain, Martin. He's been in pain for most of his life. That much, at least, you *know*.

DYSART Possibly.

HESTHER *Possibly?!* ... That cut-off little figure you just described must have been in pain for years.

DYSART (*doggedly*) Possibly.

HESTHER And you can take it away.

DYSART Still – possibly.

HESTHER Then that's enough. That simply has to be enough for you, surely?

DYSART No!

HESTHER Why not?

DYSART Because it's his.

HESTHER I don't understand.

DYSART His pain. His own. He made it.

Pause.

(*earnestly*) Look ... to go through life and call it yours – *your life* – you first have to get your own pain. Pain that's unique

66

to you. You can't just dip into the common bin and say 'That's enough!'...He's done that. All right, he's sick. He's full of misery and fear. He was dangerous, and could be again, though I doubt it. But that boy has known a passion more ferocious than I have felt in any second of my life. And let me tell you something: I envy it.

HESTHER You can't.

DYSART (*vehemently*) Don't you see? That's the Accusation! That's what his stare has been saying to me all this time. '*At least I galloped! When did you?*'...(*simply*) I'm jealous, Hesther. Jealous of Alan Strang.

HESTHER That's absurd.

DYSART Is it?...I go on about my wife. That smug woman by the fire. Have you thought of the fellow on the other side of it? The finicky, critical husband looking through his art books on mythical Greece. What worship has *he* ever known? Real worship! Without worship you shrink, it's as brutal as that...I shrank my *own* life. No one can do it for you. I settled for being pallid and provincial, out of my own eternal timidity. The old story of bluster, and do bugger-all...I imply that we can't have children: but actually, it's only me. I had myself tested behind her back. The lowest sperm count you could find. And I never told her. That's all I need – her sympathy mixed with resentment...I tell everyone Margaret's the puritan, I'm the pagan. Some pagan! Such wild returns I make to the womb of civilization. Three weeks a year in the Peleponnese, every bed booked in advance, every meal paid for by vouchers, cautious jaunts in hired Fiats, suitcase crammed with Kao-Pectate! Such a fantastic surrender to the primitive. And I use that word endlessly: 'primitive'. 'Oh, the primitive world,' I say. 'What instinctual truths were lost with it!' And while I sit there, baiting a poor unimaginative woman with the word, that freaky boy tries to conjure the reality! I sit looking at pages of centaurs trampling the soil of Argos – and outside my window he is trying to *become one*, in a Hampshire field!...I watch that woman knitting, night after night – a woman I haven't *kissed* in six years – and he stands in the dark for an hour, sucking the sweat off his God's hairy cheek! (*pause*) Then in the morning, I put away my books on the cultural shelf, close up the Kodachrome snaps of Mount Olympus, touch my reproduction statue of Dionysus for luck – and go off to hospital to treat him for insanity. Do you see?

HESTHER The boy's in pain, Martin. That's all I see. In the end ... I'm sorry.

He looks at her. Alan gets up from his bench and stealthily places an envelope in the left-hand entrance of the square, then goes back and sits with his back to the audience, as if watching television.

Hesther rises.

HESTHER That stare of his. Have you thought it might not be accusing you at all?

DYSART What then?

HESTHER Claiming you.

DYSART For what?

HESTHER (*mischievously*) A new God.

Pause.

DYSART Too conventional, for him. Finding a religion in Psychiatry is really for very ordinary patients.

She laughs.

HESTHER Maybe he just wants a new Dad. Or is that too conventional too? ... Since you're questioning your profession anyway, perhaps you ought to try it and see.

DYSART (*amused*) I'll talk to you.

HESTHER Goodbye.

She smiles, and leaves him.

26

Dysart becomes aware of the letter lying on the floor. He picks it up, opens and reads it.

ALAN (*speaking stiffly, as Dysart reads*) 'It is all true, what I said after you tapped the pencil. I'm sorry if I said different. Post Scriptum: I know why I'm in here.'

Pause.

DYSART (*calling, joyfully*) Nurse!

Nurse comes in.

NURSE Yes, Doctor?

DYSART (*trying to conceal his pleasure*) Good evening!

NURSE You're in late tonight.

DYSART Yes!... Tell me, is the Strang boy in bed yet?

NURSE Oh, no, Doctor. He's bound to be upstairs looking at television. He always watches to the last possible moment. He doesn't like going to his room at all.

DYSART You mean he's still having nightmares?

NURSE He had a bad one last night.

DYSART Would you ask him to come down here, please?

NURSE (*faint surprise*) Now?

DYSART I'd like a word with him.

NURSE (*puzzled*) Very good, Doctor.

DYSART If he's not back in his room by lights out, tell Night Nurse not to worry. I'll see he gets back to bed all right. And would you phone my home and tell my wife I may be in late?

NURSE Yes, Doctor.

DYSART Ask him to come straight away, please.

Nurse goes to the bench, taps Alan on the shoulder, whispers her message in his ear, and returns to her place. Alan stands up and pauses for a second – then steps into the square.

27

He stands in the doorway, depressed.

DYSART Hallo.
ALAN Hallo.

DYSART I got your letter. Thank you. (*pause*) Also the Post Scriptum.

ALAN (*defensively*) That's the right word. My mum told me. It's Latin for 'After-writing'.

DYSART How are you feeling?

ALAN All right.

DYSART I'm sorry I didn't see you today.

ALAN You were fed up with me.

DYSART Yes. (*pause*) Can I make it up to you now?

ALAN What d'you mean?

DYSART I thought we'd have a session.

ALAN (*startled*) Now?

DYSART Yes! At dead of night!... Better than going to sleep, isn't it?

The boy flinches.

Alan – look. Everything I say has a trick or a catch. Everything I do is a trick or a catch. That's all I know to do. But they work – and you know that. Trust me.

Pause.

ALAN You got another trick, then?

DYSART Yes.

ALAN A truth drug?

DYSART If you like.

ALAN What's it do?

DYSART Make it easier for you to talk.

ALAN Like you can't help yourself?

DYSART That's right. Like you have to speak the truth at all costs. And all of it.

Pause.

ALAN (*slyly*) Comes in a needle, doesn't it?

DYSART No.

ALAN Where is it?

DYSART (*indicating his pocket*) In here.

ALAN Let's see.

Dysart solemnly takes a bottle of pills out of his pocket.

DYSART There.

ALAN (*suspicious*) That really it?

DYSART It is... Do you want to try it?

ALAN No.

DYSART I think you do.

ALAN I don't. Not at all.

DYSART Afterwards you'd sleep. You'd have no bad dreams all
night. Probably many nights, from then on...

Pause.

ALAN How long's it take to work?

DYSART It's instant. Like coffee.

ALAN (*half believing*) It isn't!

DYSART I promise you... Well?

ALAN Can I have a fag?

DYSART Pill first. Do you want some water?

ALAN No.

*Dysart shakes one out on to his palm. Alan hesitates for a second – then
takes it and swallows it.*

DYSART Then you can chase it down with this. Sit down.

He offers him a cigarette, and lights it for him.

ALAN (*nervous*) What happens now?

DYSART We wait for it to work.

ALAN What'll I feel first?

DYSART Nothing much. After a minute, about a hundred green
snakes should come out of that cupboard singing the Halle-
lujah Chorus.

ALAN (*annoyed*) *I'm serious!*

DYSART (*earnestly*) You'll feel nothing. Nothing's going to happen now but what you want to happen. You're not going to
say anything to me but what you want to say. Just relax. Lie
back and finish your fag.

Alan stares at him. Then accepts the situation, and lies back.

DYSART Good boy.

ALAN I bet this room's heard some funny things.

DYSART It certainly has.

ALAN I like it.

DYSART This room?

71

ALAN Don't you?

DYSART Well, there's not much to like, is there?

ALAN How long am I going to be in here?

DYSART It's hard to say. I quite see you want to leave.

ALAN No.

DYSART You don't?

ALAN Where would I go?

DYSART Home....

The boy looks at him. Dysart crosses and sits on the rail upstage, his feet on the bench. A pause.

Actually, I'd like to leave this room and never see it again in my life.

ALAN (*surprise*) Why?

DYSART I've been in it too long.

ALAN Where would you go?

DYSART Somewhere.

ALAN Secret?

DYSART Yes. There's a sea – a great sea – I love . . . It's where the Gods used to go to bathe.

ALAN What Gods?

DYSART The old ones. Before they died.

ALAN Gods don't die.

DYSART Yes, they do.

Pause.

There's a village I spent one night in, where I'd like to live. It's all white.

ALAN How would you Nosey Parker, though? You wouldn't have a room for it any more.

DYSART I wouldn't mind. I don't actually enjoy being a Nosey Parker, you know.

ALAN Then why do it?

DYSART Because you're unhappy.

ALAN So are you.

Dysart looks at him sharply. Alan sits up in alarm.

Oooh, I didn't mean that!

DYSART Didn't you?

ALAN Here – is that how it works? Things just slip out, not feeling anything?

DYSART That's right.

ALAN But it's so quick!

DYSART I told you: it's instant.

ALAN (*delighted*) It's wicked, isn't it? I mean, you can say anything under it.

DYSART Yes.

ALAN Ask me a question.

DYSART Tell me about Jill.

Pause. The boy turns away.

ALAN There's nothing to tell.

DYSART Nothing?

ALAN No.

DYSART Well, for example – is she pretty? You've never described her.

ALAN She's all right.

DYSART What colour hair?

ALAN Dunno.

DYSART Is it long or short?

ALAN Dunno.

DYSART (*lightly*) You must know that.

ALAN I don't remember. *I don't!*

Dysart rises and comes down to him. He takes the cigarette out of his hand.

DYSART (*firmly*) Lie back....Now listen. You have to do this. And now. You are going to tell me everything that happened with this girl. And not just *tell* me – *show* me. Act it out, if you like – even more than you did when I tapped the pencil. I want you to feel free to do absolutely anything in this room. The pill will help you. I will help you... Now, where does she live?

A long pause.

ALAN (*tight*) Near the stables. About a mile.

Dysart steps down out of the square as Jill enters it. He sits again on the downstage bench.

28

The light grows warmer.

JILL It's called The China Pantry.
She comes down and sits casually on the rail. Her manner is open and lightly provocative. During these scenes Alan acts directly with her, and never looks over at Dysart when he replies to him.

When Daddy disappeared, she was left without a bean. She had to earn her own living. I must say she did jolly well, considering she was never trained in business.

DYSART What do you mean, 'disappeared'?

ALAN (*to Dysart*) He ran off. No one ever saw him again.

JILL Just left a note on her dressing table saying 'Sorry. I've had it.' Just like that. She never got over it. It turned her right off men. All my dates have to be sort of secret. I mean, she knows about them, but I can't ever bring anyone back home. She's so rude to them.

ALAN (*to Dysart*) She was always looking.

DYSART At you?

ALAN (*to Dysart*) Saying stupid things.

She jumps off the bench.

JILL You've got super eyes.

ALAN (*to Dysart*) Anyway, *she* was the one who had them.

She sits next to him. Embarrassed, the boy tries to move away as far as he can.

JILL There was an article in the paper last week saying what points about boys fascinate girls. They said Number One is bottoms. I think it's eyes every time ... They fascinate you too, don't they?

ALAN Me?

JILL (*sly*) Or is it only horse's eyes?

ALAN (*startled*) What d'you mean?

JILL I saw you staring into Nugget's eyes yesterday for ages. I spied on you through the door!

ALAN (*hotly*) There must have been something in it!

JILL You're a real Man of Mystery, aren't you?

ALAN (*to Dysart*) Sometimes, it was like she knew.

DYSART Did you ever hint?

ALAN (*to Dysart*) Course not!

JILL I love horses' eyes. The way you can see yourself in them. D'you find them sexy?

ALAN (*outraged*) What?!

JILL Horses.

ALAN Don't be daft!

He springs up, and away from her.

JILL Girls do. I mean, they go through a period when they pat them and kiss them a lot. I know *I* did. I suppose it's just a substitute, really.

ALAN (*to Dysart*) That kind of thing, all the time. Until one night...

DYSART Yes? What?

ALAN (*to Dysart: defensively*) She did it! Not me. It was her idea, the whole thing!...She got me into it!

DYSART What are you saying? 'One night': go on from there.

A pause.

ALAN (*to Dysart*) Saturday night. We were just closing up.

JILL How would you like to take me out?

ALAN What?

JILL (*coolly*) How would you like to take me out tonight?

ALAN I've got to go home.

JILL What for?

He tries to escape upstage.

ALAN They expect me.

JILL Ring up and say you're going out.

ALAN I can't.

JILL Why?

ALAN They expect me.

JILL Look. Either we go out together and have some fun, or you go back to your boring home, *as usual*, and I go back to mine. That's the situation, isn't it?

ALAN Well...where would we go?

75

JILL The pictures! There's a skinflick over in Winchester! I've never seen one, have you?

ALAN No.

JILL Wouldn't you like to? *I* would. All those heavy Swedes, panting at each other!... What d'you say?

ALAN (*grinning*) Yeh!...

JILL Good!...

He turns away.

DYSART Go on, please.

He steps off the square.

ALAN (*to Dysart*) I'm tired now!

DYSART Come on now. You can't stop there.

He storms round the circle to Dysart, and faces him directly.

ALAN I'm *tired!* I want to go to bed!

DYSART (*sharply*) Well, you can't. I want to hear about the film.

ALAN (*hostile*) Hear what?... *What?*... It was bloody awful!

The actors playing horses come swiftly on to the square, dressed in sports coats or raincoats. They move the benches to be parallel with the audience, and sit on them – staring out front.

DYSART Why?

ALAN Nosey Parker!

DYART *Why?*

ALAN *Because!*... Well – we went into the Cinema!

29

A burst of rock music, instantly fading down. Lights darken.

Alan re-enters the square. Jill rises and together they grope their way to the downstage bench, as if in a dark auditorium.

ALAN (*to Dysart*) The whole place was full of men. Jill was the only girl.

They push by a patron seated at the end, and sit side by side, staring up at the invisible screen, located above the heads of the main audience.

A spotlight hits the boy's face.

We sat down and the film came on. It was daft. Nothing happened for ages. There was this girl Brita, who was sixteen. She went to stay in this house, where there was an older boy. He kept giving her looks, but she ignored him completely. In the end she took a shower. She went into the bathroom and took off all her clothes. The lot. Very slowly.... What she didn't know was the boy was looking through the door all the time.... (*he starts to become excited*) It was fantastic! The water fell on her breasts, bouncing down her....

Frank steps into the square furtively from the back, hat in hand, and stands looking about for a place.

DYSART Was that the first time you'd seen a girl naked?

ALAN (*to Dysart*) Yes! You couldn't see everything, though.... (*looking about him*) All round me they were all looking. All the men – staring up like they were in church. Like they were a sort of congregation. And then – (*he sees his father*) *Ah!*

At the same instant Frank sees him.

FRANK Alan!

ALAN God!

JILL What is it?

ALAN *Dad!*

JILL *Where?*

ALAN At the back! *He saw me!*

JILL You sure?

ALAN Yes!

FRANK (*calling*) Alan!

ALAN Oh God!

He tries to hide his face in the girl's shoulder. His father comes down the aisle towards him.

FRANK Alan! You can hear me! Don't pretend!

PATRONS *Sssh!*

FRANK (*approaching the row of seats*) Do I have to come and fetch you out? ... Do I? ...

Cries of 'Sssh!' and 'Shut up!'

Do I, Alan?

ALAN (*through gritted teeth*) Oh fuck!

He gets up as the noise increases. Jill gets up too and follows him.

DYSART You went?

ALAN (*to Dysart*) What else could I do? He kept shouting. Everyone was saying Shut up!

They go out, right, through the group of Patrons – who rise protesting as they pass, quickly replace the benches and leave the square.

Dysart enters it.

30

Light brightens from the cinema, but remains cold: streets at night.

The three walk round the circle downstage in a line: Frank leading, wearing his hat. He halts in the middle of the left rail, and stands staring straight ahead of him, rigid with embarrassment. Alan is very agitated.

ALAN (*to Dysart*) We went into the street, all three of us. It was weird. We just stood there by the bus stop – like we were three people in a queue, and we didn't know each other. Dad was all white and sweaty. He didn't look at us at all. It must have gone on for about five minutes. I tried to speak. I said – (*to his father*) I – I – I've never been there before. Honest... Never... (*to Dysart*) He didn't seem to hear. Jill tried.

JILL It's true, Mr Strang. It wasn't Alan's idea to go there. It was mine.

ALAN (*to Dysart*) He just went on staring, straight ahead. It was awful.

JILL I'm not shocked by films like that. I think they're just silly.

ALAN (*to Dysart*) The bus wouldn't come. We just stood and stood.... Then suddenly he spoke.

Frank takes off his hat.

FRANK (*stiffly*) I'd like you to know something. Both of you. I came here tonight to see the Manager. He asked me to call on him for business purposes. I happen to be a printer, Miss. A picture house needs posters. That's entirely why I'm here. To discuss posters. While I was waiting I happened to glance in, that's all. I can only say I'm going to complain to the council. I had no idea they showed films like this. I'm certainly going to refuse my services.

JILL (*kindly*) Yes, of course.

FRANK So long as that's understood.

ALAN (*to Dysart*) Then the bus came along.

FRANK Come along, now Alan.

He moves away downstage.

ALAN No.

FRANK (*turning*) No fuss, please. Say Goodnight to the young lady.

ALAN (*timid but firm*) No. I'm stopping here... I've got to see her home... It's proper.

Pause.

FRANK (*as dignified as possible*) Very well. I'll see you when you choose to return. Very well then... Yes...

He walks back to his original seat, next to his wife. He stares across the square at his son – who stares back at him. Then, slowly, he sits.

ALAN (*to Dysart*) And he got in, and we didn't. He sat down and looked at me through the glass. And I saw...

DYSART (*soft*) What?

ALAN (*to Dysart*) His face. It was scared.

DYSART Of you?

ALAN (*to Dysart*) It was terrible. We had to walk home. Four miles. I got the shakes.

DYSART You were scared too?

ALAN (*to Dysart*) It was like a hole had been drilled in my tummy. A hole – right here. And the air was getting in!

He starts to walk upstage, round the circle.

31

The girl stays still.

JILL (*aware of other people looking*) Alan . . .

ALAN (*to Dysart*) People kept turning round in the street to look.

JILL Alan!

ALAN (*to Dysart*) I kept seeing him, just as he drove off. Scared of me. . . . And me scared of *him*. . . . I kept thinking – all those airs he put on! . . . 'Receive my meaning. Improve your mind!' . . . All those nights he said he'd be in late. 'Keep my supper hot, Dora!' 'Your poor father: he works so hard!' . . . Bugger! Old bugger! . . . Filthy old bugger!

He stops, clenching his fists.

JILL Hey! Wait for me!

She runs after him. He waits.

What are you thinking about?

ALAN Nothing.

JILL Mind my own beeswax?

She laughs.

ALAN (*to Dysart*) And suddenly she began to laugh.

JILL I'm sorry. But it's pretty funny, when you think of it.

ALAN (*bewildered*) What?

JILL Catching him like that! I mean, it's terrible – but it's very funny.

ALAN Yeh!

He turns from her.

JILL No, wait! . . . I'm sorry. I know you're upset. But it's not the end of the world, is it? I mean, what was he doing? Only what we were. Watching a silly film. It's a case of like father like son, I'd say! . . . I mean, when that girl was taking a shower, you were pretty interested, weren't you?

He turns round and looks at her.

We keep saying old people are square. Then when they suddenly aren't – we don't like it!

DYSART What did you think about that?

ALAN (*to Dysart*) I don't know. I kept looking at all the people in the street. They were mostly men coming out of pubs. I suddenly thought – *they all do it! All of them!* . . . They're not just Dads – they're people with pricks! . . . And Dad – he's not just Dad either. He's a man with a prick too. You know, I'd never thought about it.

Pause.

We went into the country.

He walks again. Jill follows. They turn the corner and come downstage, right.

We kept walking. I just thought about Dad, and how he was nothing special – just a poor old sod on his own.

He stops.

(*to Jill: realising it*) Poor old sod!

JILL That's right!

ALAN (*grappling with it*) I mean, what else has he got? . . . He's got mum, of course, but well – she – she – she—

JILL She doesn't give him anything?

ALAN That's right. I bet you . . . She doesn't give him anything. That's right . . . That's really right! . . . She likes Ladies and Gentlemen. Do you understand what I mean?

JILL (*mischievously*) Ladies and gentlemen aren't naked?

ALAN That's right! Never! . . . *Never!* That would be disgusting! She'd have to put bowler hats on them! . . . Jodhpurs!

She laughs.

DYSART Was that the first time you ever thought anything like that about your mother? . . . I mean, that she was unfair to your dad?

ALAN (*to Dysart*) Absolutely!

DYSART How did you feel?

ALAN (*to Dysart*) Sorry. I mean for him. Poor old sod, that's what I felt – he's just like me! He hates ladies and gents just like me! Posh things – and la-di-da. He goes off by himself at night, and does his own secret thing which no one'll know about, just like me! There's no difference – he's just the same as me – just the same!—

He stops in distress, then bolts back a little upstage.

Christ!

DYSART *(sternly)* Go on.

ALAN *(to Dysart)* I can't.

DYSART Of course you can. You're doing wonderfully.

ALAN *(to Dysart)* No, please. *Don't make me!*

DYSART *(firm)* Don't think: just answer. You were happy at that second, weren't you? When you realised about your dad. How lots of people have secrets, not just you?

ALAN *(to Dysart)* Yes.

DYSART You felt sort of free, didn't you? I mean, free to do anything?

ALAN *(to Dysart, looking at Jill)* Yes!

DYSART What was she doing?

ALAN *(to Dysart)* Holding my hand.

DYSART And that was good?

ALAN *(to Dysart)* Oh, yes!

DYSART Remember what you thought. *As if it's happening to you now. This very moment* . . . What's in your head?

ALAN *(to Dysart)* Her eyes. *She's* the one with eyes! . . . I keep looking at them, because I really want—

DYSART To look at her breasts?

ALAN *(to Dysart)* Yes.

DYSART Like in the film.

ALAN *(to Dysart)* Yes . . . Then she starts to scratch my hand.

JILL You're really very nice, you know that?

ALAN *(to Dysart)* Moving her nails on the back. Her face so warm. Her eyes.

DYSART You want her very much?

ALAN *(to Dysart)* Yes . . .

JILL I love your eyes.

She kisses him.

(whispering) Let's go!

ALAN Where?

JILL I know a place. It's right near here.

ALAN Where?

JILL Surprise!... Come on!

She darts away round the circle, across the stage and up the left side.
Come *on!*

ALAN (*to Dysart*) She runs ahead. I follow. And then – and then—!

He halts.

DYSART What?

ALAN (*to Dysart*) I see what she means.

DYSART What?... Where are you?... Where has she taken you?

ALAN (*to Jill*) *The Stables?*

JILL Of course!

32

Chorus makes a warning hum.

The horses-actors enter, and ceremonially put on their masks – first raising them high above their heads. Nugget stands in the central tunnel.

ALAN (*recoiling*) No!

JILL Where else? They're perfect!

ALAN No!

He turns his head from her.

JILL Or do you want to go home now and face your dad?

ALAN No!

JILL Then come on!

He edges nervously past the horse standing at the left, which turns its neck and even moves a challenging step after him.

ALAN Why not your place?

JILL I can't. Mother doesn't like me bringing back boys. I told you.... Anyway, the Barn's better.

ALAN No!

JILL All that straw. It's cosy.

ALAN No.

JILL *Why not?*

ALAN Them!

JILL Dalton will be in bed ... What's the matter? ... Don't you want to?

ALAN (*aching to*) Yes!

JILL So?

ALAN (*desperate*) *Them! ... Them! ...*

JILL *Who?*

ALAN (*low*) Horses.

JILL *Horses?* ... You're really dotty, aren't you? ... What do you mean?

He starts shaking.

Oh, you're freezing ... Let's get under the straw. You'll be warm there.

ALAN (*pulling away*) No!

JILL What on earth's the matter with you? ...

Silence. He won't look at her.

Look, if the sight of horses offends you, my lord, we can just shut the door. You won't have to see them. All right?

DYSART What door is that? In the barn?

ALAN (*to Dysart*) Yes.

DYSART So what do you do? You go in?

ALAN (*to Dysart*) Yes.

33

A rich light falls.

Furtively Alan enters the square from the top end, and Jill follows. The horses on the circle retire out of sight on either side. Nugget retreats up the tunnel and stands where he can just be glimpsed in the dimness.

DYSART Into the Temple? The Holy of Holies?

ALAN (*to Dysart: desperate*) What else can I do? ... I can't say! I can't tell her ... (*to Jill*) Shut it tight.

JILL All right ... You're crazy.

ALAN Lock it.

JILL Lock?

ALAN Yes.

JILL It's just an old door. What's the matter with you? They're in their boxes. They can't get out... Are you all right?

ALAN Why?

JILL You look weird.

ALAN *Lock it!*

JILL Ssssh! D'you want to wake up Dalton?... Stay there, idiot.

She mimes locking a heavy door, upstage.

DYSART Describe the barn, please.

ALAN (*walking round it: to Dysart*) Large room. Straw everywhere. Some tools... (*as if picking it up off the rail where he left it in Act One*) A hoof pick!...

He 'drops' it hastily, and dashes away from the spot.

DYSART *Go on.*

ALAN (*to Dysart*) At the end this big door. Behind it—

DYSART Horses.

ALAN (*to Dysart*) Yes.

DYSART How many?

ALAN (*to Dysart*) Six.

DYSART Jill closes the door so you can't see them?

ALAN (*to Dysart*) Yes.

DYSART And then?... What happens now?... Come on, Alan. Show me.

JILL See, it's all shut. There's just us... Let's sit down. Come on.

They sit together on the same bench, left.

Hallo.

ALAN (*quickly*) Hallo.

She kisses him lightly. He responds. Suddenly a faint trampling of hooves, off-stage, makes him jump up.

JILL What is it?

He turns his head upstage, listening.

Relax. There's no one there. Come here.

85

She touches his hand. He turns to her again.

You're very gentle. I love that...

ALAN So are you... I mean...

He kisses her spontaneously. The hooves trample again, harder. He breaks away from her abruptly towards the upstage corner.

JILL (*rising*) What is it?

ALAN Nothing!

She moves towards him. He turns and moves past her. He is clearly distressed. She contemplates him for a moment.

JILL (*gently*) Take your sweater off.

ALAN What?

JILL I will, if you will.

He stares at her. A pause.

She lifts her sweater over her head: he watches – then unzips his. They each remove their shoes, their socks, and their jeans. Then they look at each other diagonally across the square, in which the light is gently increasing.

ALAN You're... You're very...

JILL So are you.... (*pause*) Come here.

He goes to her. She comes to him. They meet in the middle, and hold each other, and embrace.

ALAN (*to Dysart*) She put her mouth in mine. It was lovely! *Oh, it was lovely!*

They burst into giggles. He lays her gently on the floor in the centre of the square, and bends over her eagerly.

Suddenly the noise of Equus fills the place. Hooves smash on wood. Alan straightens up, rigid. He stares straight ahead of him over the prone body of the girl.

DYSART Yes, what happened then, Alan?

ALAN (*to Dysart: brutally*) I put it in her!

DYSART Yes?

ALAN (*to Dysart*) I put it in her.

DYSART You did?

ALAN(*to Dysart*) Yes!

DYSART Was it easy?

ALAN (*to Dysart*) Yes.

DYSART Describe it.

ALAN (*to Dysart*) I told you.

DYSART More exactly.

ALAN (*to Dysart*) I put it in her!

DYSART Did you?

ALAN (*to Dysart*) All the way!

DYSART Did you, Alan?

ALAN (*to Dysart*) All the way. I shoved it. I put it in her all the way.

DYSART Did you?

ALAN (*to Dysart*) Yes!

DYSART Did you?

ALAN (*to Dysart*) Yes!... Yes!

DYSART Give me the TRUTH!... Did you?... *Honestly?*

ALAN (*to Dysart*) Fuck off!

He collapses, lying upstage on his face. Jill lies on her back motionless, her head downstage, her arms extended behind her. A pause.

DYSART (*gently*) What was it? You couldn't? Though you wanted to very much?

ALAN (*to Dysart*) I couldn't... see her.

DYSART What do you mean?

ALAN (*to Dysart*) Only Him. Every time I kissed her – *He* was in the way.

DYSART Who?

Alan turns on his back.

ALAN (*to Dysart*) You *know* who!... When I touched her, I felt *Him*. Under me... His side, waiting for my hand... His flanks... I refused him. I looked. I looked right at her... and I couldn't do it. When I shut my eyes, I saw Him at once. The streaks on his belly... (*with more desperation*) I couldn't feel *her* flesh at all! I wanted the foam off his neck. His sweaty hide. Not flesh. *Hide! Horse-hide!*... Then I couldn't even kiss her.

Jill sits up.

JILL What is it?

ALAN (*dodging her hand*) No!

He scrambles up and crouches in the corner against the rails, like a little beast in a cage.

JILL Alan!

ALAN Stop it!

Jill gets up.

JILL It's all right... It's all right... Don't worry about it. It often happens – honest... There's nothing wrong. I don't mind, you know... I don't at all.

He dashes past her downstage.

Alan, look at me... Alan?... Alan!

He collapses again by the rail.

ALAN Get out!...

JILL What?

ALAN (*soft*) Out!

JILL There's nothing wrong: believe me! It's very common.

ALAN *Get out!*

He snatches up the invisible pick.

GET OUT!

JILL Put that down!

ALAN Leave me alone!

JILL Put that down, Alan. It's very dangerous. Go on, please – drop it.

He 'drops' it, and turns from her.

ALAN You ever tell anyone. Just you tell...

JILL Who do you think I am?... I'm your friend – Alan...

She goes towards him.

Listen: you don't have to do anything. Try to realize that. Nothing at all. Why don't we just lie here together in the straw. And talk.

ALAN (*low*) Please...

JILL Just talk.

ALAN *Please!*

JILL All right, I'm going... Let me put my clothes on first.

She dresses, hastily.

ALAN You tell anyone!... Just tell and see....

JILL *Oh, stop it!*... I wish you could believe me. It's not in

the least important.
Pause.

Anyway, I won't say anything. You know that. You know I won't....

Pause. He stands with his back to her.

Goodnight, then, Alan.... I wish – I really wish—

He turns on her, hissing. His face is distorted – possessed. In horrified alarm she turns – fumbles the door open – leaves the barn – shuts the door hard behind her, and dashes up the tunnel out of sight, past the barely visible figure of Nugget.

34

Alan stands alone, and naked.

A faint humming and drumming. The boy looks about him in growing terror.

DYSART What?

ALAN (*to Dysart*) He was there. Through the door. The door was shut, but he was there!... He'd seen everything. I could hear him. He was laughing.

DYSART Laughing?

ALAN (*to Dysart*) Mocking!... *Mocking!*...

Standing downstage he stares up towards the tunnel. A great silence weighs on the square.

(*to the silence: terrified*) Friend ... Equus the Kind ... The Merciful!... *Forgive me!*...

Silence.

It wasn't me. Not really me. *Me!*... Forgive me!... Take me back again! Please!... PLEASE!

He kneels on the downstage lip of the square, still facing the door, huddling in fear.

I'll never do it again. I swear ... I swear!...

Silence.

(*in a moan*) *Please!!!*...

DYSART And He? What does He say?

ALAN (*to Dysart: whispering*) 'Mine!... You're mine!... I am yours and you are mine!'... Then I see his eyes. They are rolling!

Nugget begins to advance slowly, with relentless hooves, down the central tunnel.

'I see you. I see you. Always! Everywhere! Forever!'

DYSART Kiss anyone and I will see?

ALAN (*to Dysart*) Yes!

DYSART Lie with anyone and I will see?

ALAN (*to Dysart*) Yes!

DYSART And you will fail! Forever and ever you will *fail!* You will see ME – and you will FAIL!

The boy turns round, hugging himself in pain. From the sides two more horses converge with Nugget on the rails. Their hooves stamp angrily. The equus Noise is heard more terribly.

The Lord thy God is a Jealous God. He sees you. He sees you forever and ever, Alan. He sees you!... *He sees you!*

ALAN (*in terror*) Eyes!... White eyes – never closed! Eyes like flames – coming – coming!... God seest! God seest!... NO!...

Pause. He steadies himself. The stage begins to blacken.

(*quieter*) No more. No more, Equus.

He gets up. He goes to the bench. He takes up the invisible pick. He moves slowly upstage towards Nugget, concealing the weapon behind his naked back, in the growing darkness. He stretches out his hand and fondles Nugget's mask.

(*gently*) Equus... Noble Equus... Faithful and True... Godslave... Thou—God—Seest—NOTHING!

He stabs out Nugget's eyes. The horse stamps in agony. A great screaming begins to fill the theatre, growing ever louder. Alan dashes at the other two horses and blinds them too, stabbing over the rails. Their metal hooves join in the stamping.

Relentlessly, as this happens, three more horses appear in cones of light: not naturalistic animals like the first three, but dreadful creatures out of nightmare. Their eyes flare – their nostrils flare – their mouths flare. They are archetypal images – judging, punishing, pitiless. They do not halt at the rail, but invade the square. As they trample at him, the boy leaps desperately at them, jumping high and naked in the dark, slashing at their heads with arms upraised.

The screams increase. The other horses follow into the square. The whole place is filled with cannoning, blinded horses – and the boy dodging among them, avoiding their slashing hooves as best he can. Finally they plunge off into darkness and away out of sight. The noise dies abruptly, and all we hear is Alan yelling in hysteria as he collapses on the ground – stabbing at his own eyes with the invisible pick.

ALAN Find me!...Find me!...Find me!...

KILL ME!...KILL ME!...

35

The light changes quickly back to brightness.

Dysart enters swiftly, hurls a blanket on the left bench, and rushes over to Alan. The boy is having convulsions on the floor. Dysart grabs his hands, forces them from his eyes, scoops him up in his arms and carries him over to the bench. Alan hurls his arms round Dysart and clings to him, gasping and kicking his legs in a dreadful frenzy.

Dysart lays him down and presses his head back on the bench. He keeps talking – urgently talking – soothing the agony as he can.

DYSART Here...Here...Ssssh...Ssssh...Calm now ... Lie back. *Just lie back!* Now breathe in deep. Very deep. In...
Out...In...Out... That's it. ...In. Out...*In...Out...*

The boy's breath is drawn into his body with a harsh rasping sound, which slowly grows less. Dysart puts the blanket over him.

Keep it going...That's a good boy... Very good boy....
It's all over now, Alan. It's all over. He'll go away now.
You'll never see him again, I promise. You'll have no more bad dreams. No more awful nights. Think of that!... You are going to be well. I'm going to make you well, I promise you.... You'll be here for a while, but I'll be here too, so it won't be so bad. Just trust me ...

He stands upright. The boy lies still.

Sleep now. Have a good long sleep. You've earned it . . .
Sleep. Just sleep. . . I'm going to make you well.

*He steps backwards into the centre of the square. The light brightens
some more.*

A pause.

DYSART I'm lying to you, Alan. He won't really go that easily.
Just clop away from you like a nice old nag. Oh, no! When
Equus leaves – if he leaves at all – it will be with your intes-
tines in his teeth. And I don't stock replacements . . . If you
knew anything, you'd get up this minute and run from me
fast as you could.

Hesther speaks from her place.

HESTHER The boy's in pain, Martin.

DYSART Yes.

HESTHER And you can take it away.

DYSART Yes.

HESTHER Then that has to be enough for you, surely? . . . In
the end!

DYSART (*crying out*) *All right! I'll take it away!* He'll be delivered
from madness. *What then?* He'll feel himself acceptable! *What
then?* Do you think feelings like his can be simply re-attached,
like plasters? Stuck on to other objects we select? *Look at
him!* . . . My desire might be to make this boy an ardent husband – a caring citizen – a worshipper of abstract and uni-
fying God. My achievement, however, is more likely to make
a ghost! . . . Let me tell you exactly what I'm going to do to
him!

*He steps out of the square and walks round the upstage end of it, storm-
ing at the audience.*

I'll heal the rash on his body. I'll erase the welts cut into his
mind by flying manes. When that's done, I'll set him on a
nice mini-scooter and send him puttering off into the Normal world where animals are treated *properly*: made extinct,
or put into servitude, or tethered all their lives in dim light,
just to feed it! I'll give him the good Normal world where
we're tethered beside them – blinking our nights away in a

non-stop drench of cathode-ray over our shrivelling heads! I'll take away his Field of Ha Ha, and give him Normal places for his ecstasy – multi-lane highways driven through the guts of cities, extinguishing Place altogether, *even the idea of Place!* He'll trot on his metal pony tamely through the concrete evening – and one thing I promise you: he will never touch hide again! With any luck his private parts will come to feel as plastic to him as the products of the factory to which he will almost certainly be sent. Who knows? He may even come to find sex funny. Smirky funny. Bit of grunt funny. Trampled and furtive and entirely in control. Hopefully, he'll feel nothing at his fork but Approved Flesh. *I doubt, however, with much passion!* . . . Passion, you see, can be destroyed by a doctor. It cannot be created.

He addresses Alan directly, in farewell.

You won't gallop any more, Alan. Horses will be quite safe. You'll save your pennies every week, till you can change that scooter in for a car, and put the odd fifty p on the gee-gees, quite forgetting that they were ever anything more to you than bearers of little profits and little losses. You will, however, be without pain. More or less completely without pain.

Pause.

He speaks directly to the theatre, standing by the motionless body of Alan Strang, under the blanket.

And now for me it never stops: that voice of Equus out of the cave – 'Why Me? . . . Why Me? . . . Account for Me!' . . . All right – I surrender! I say it! . . . In an ultimate sense I cannot know what I do in this place – yet I do ultimate things. Essentially I cannot know what I do – yet I do essential things. Irreversible, terminal things. I stand in the dark with a pick in my hand, striking at heads!

He moves away from Alan, back to the downstage bench, and finally sits.

I need – more desperately than my children need me – a way of seeing in the dark. What way is this? . . . *What dark is this?* . . . I cannot call it ordained of God: I can't get that far.

Glossary: reading the text

Author's notes on the play

xxii *Chorus*   organised band of singers or dancers, especially in Greek tragedy representing interested spectators and employed to explain the actions, express sympathy with characters and draw morals.

xxiii *blinkers*   leather screens on a horse's bridle preventing it from seeing sideways.

mimetically   by copying or imitation.

Act 1, scenes 1 to 7

3 *schizophrenic*   person suffering from a mental disease marked by disconnection between thoughts, feelings and actions.

catatonia   state of inertia. Catatonic schizophrenia is a kind of mental illness in which the sufferer can stay in a state of absolute immobility for a long time.

bench   in the British judicial system this is the magistrate's or judge's seat in a court. Hesther is probably a magistrate. A magistrate is usually an unpaid layperson appointed to try minor offences.

Polynesian   inhabitant of islands in the central and west Pacific including Hawaii and New Zealand.

4 *Spanish fly*   dried beetle formerly used in medicine and thought to have aphrodisiac qualities.

6 *Doublemint*   brand of chewing gum.

Martini   popular vermouth drink. This and the Doublemint gum are both featured in advertising jingles which were well known at the time that this play was first produced. Alan's repetition of these advertising jingles is used by him as a means of evasion; they screen him from Dysart's probing questions. They also suggest that Alan is highly responsive to the influences which surround him.

1 How successful is the opening of the play in gaining the audience's attention and at engaging its curiosity?

2 What are your initial impressions of Alan and Dysart?

3 How does the audience's attitude towards Alan develop during these opening scenes? To what extent can we sympathise with him in spite of our knowledge of what he has done?

4 What are the various ways in which we learn about Alan during these scenes?

5 What has been learned of Alan's motives for blinding the horses by the end of scene 7?

6 Does Alan appear to be mentally unbalanced? If so, in what ways?

7 What is your first impression of Alan's father? What are the reasons for introducing him into the play at this point?

8 How does Shaffer characterise the Strangs' relationship?

Act 1, scenes 8 to 11

7 *lav* common abbreviation for the lavatory.

8 *Homeric* Homer, probable author of **The Iliad** and **The Odyssey;** Greek epic poet of classical times.

Agamemnon in Greek legend, King of Argos and commander of the Greek army which besieged Troy. He was murdered on his return from Troy by his wife Clytemnestra and her lover Aegisthus. The mask referred to is the gold funeral mask wrongly believed to have been that of Agamemnon.

Mycenae   city of ancient Greece in the plain of Argos in the Peloponnese region.

9 *menopause*   period in a woman's life, generally between forty and fifty, at which menstruation and hence fertility ceases. This image serves to point up Dysart's feeling that his career has reached its end and that what he does is of no value.

13 *Karl Marx*   nineteenth-century German philosopher, economist and revolutionary social theorist. His view of religion was that it kept the working classes in their place at the bottom of society because it taught them to be happy with their lot.

15 '*He saith among the trumpets, Ha, ha.*'   from Job 40: 19–25.

> *Hast thou given the horse strength? hast thou clothed his neck with thunder? Canst thou make him afraid as a grasshopper? the glory of his nostrils is terrible.*
>
> *He paweth in the valley, and rejoiceth in his strength: he goeth on to meet the armed men.*
>
> *He mocketh at fear, and is not affrighted; neither turneth he back for the sword.*
>
> *The quiver rattleth against him, the glittering spear and the shield.*
>
> *He swalloweth the ground with the fierceness and rage: neither believeth he that it is the sound of the trumpet.*
>
> *He saith among the trumpets, Ha ha; And he smelleth the battle afar off, The thunder of the captains, and the shouting.*

This is an important passage for the power of its poetry in suggesting the depth of Alan's feeling and also because it establishes Alan's 'god' as being Old Testament in character. We are dealing with a world in which there can be no mercy for sinners. This section is full of images of violence and blood which would be very likely to stimulate Alan's imagination. The audience are presented with an adolescent's mind which is a strange mixture of contemporary advertisements and archaic snippets from the Bible.

The Book of Job   chapter in the Old Testament, probably written in
the fourth century BC. Its hero is a wealthy man, whose patience
and exemplary piety are tried by dire and undeserved misfortunes
and who, in spite of bitter lamentations, remains finally confident
in the goodness of God. (Hence the name is associated with
being long-suffering and patient in the face of misfortune.)

18 *atheist*   person who either does not believe in a god, or who
positively denies the very possibility of its existence. Alan's father's
rejection of religion is based on his view that it has damaged his
son's mental health.

20 *truculent*   aggressive, savage or harsh.

1   How deep an understanding do we have of Alan and his
problems by the end of this group of scenes?

2   What are the significant influences in Alan's childhood which
have driven him towards a worship of horses?

3   In what ways is Dysart beginning to develop as a character in
his own right – instead of being simply a kind of detective?

4   How does Shaffer develop the horse imagery in these scenes?

5   Explain the importance of the two pictures in Alan's
emotional development.

6   Why won't Frank allow his son to watch television?

7   What verbal strategies does Alan employ to evade Dysart's
questions and how does the psychiatrist respond?

8   What different methods does the playwright use to tell the
story of Alan's childhood?

Act 1, scenes 12 to 16

34 *begat*   to procreate or have children. In the early books in the Old Testament, there are often lists of names, family trees or genealogical tables. It is these lists which Alan's mother was always reading to him when he was little. Alan's own genealogical list traces Equus's family tree and it reveals how his obsession with horses is mixed up with his sexually repressed upbringing. Prince (the name of the horse in the story told to him by his mother) suggests the sound of Prance, which describes the springing walk of a horse. This leads – by sound association – to Prankus which suggests that Alan's childhood activities were naughty, a prank. Flankus is reminiscent of the word flank or the horse's body. The flank, being the part of the horse whipped by the rider leads us to Spankus. This suggests the idea of a naughty child being punished by having its bottom smacked (spanked) and the more general idea of flagellation as a perversion; the 'bad sex' which Alan's father refers to on page 18. The next name in the genealogy reinforces the idea that Alan's fantasies are to do with masturbation; spunk being a slang word for 'semen'. The close interlinking of ideas relating to repression, childhood punishment and sexuality suggest a Freudian view of Alan's mental problems.

Sigmund Freud, an Austrian psychiatrist, has been enormously influential in the world of psychiatry for his view that repression of infantile sexuality is the root of neurosis in adults. Dysart is clearly influenced by Freud because he investigates Alan's mental problems through an exploration of his childhood influences, particularly those of his parents.

Genealogy   a kind of pedigree, a description of the development of a species by listing all the individuals from the start to the end.

35 *Ek . . . wus*   Dysart belatedly realises the significance of the noises Alan made in his dreams earlier in Act 1, scene 6.

Alan in mime begins to thrash himself once more Alan's flagellation is coupled with his intense sexual repression. Flagellation has been used both in the name of religion as a means to deny the body's demands for pleasure and, in completely the opposite way to stimulate sexual activity.

36 *obliquely* not going straight to the point, roundabout. There is surely a little intentional irony here: Frank is unable to live up the meaning of his name ('frank' meaning candid or open) and finds himself unable to be 'frank' with his son about sex. Frank is therefore seen as being largely responsible for his son's sexual repression as a child and subsequent neurosis in adolescence.

41 *dandy . . . curry-comb* the former is a stiff brush and the latter a type of comb used for grooming horses.

---

1   In what ways does Dalton's information contribute to our understanding of Alan?

2   What aspects of horses excite and interest Alan?

3   Do you think Alan is closer to his mother or his father?

4   What do you think is the dramatic significance of Jill, stable-girl?

5   What have Dysart's revelations about his marriage to do with Alan's story?

6   What part does Hesther play in these scenes?

7   In what ways does Dysart find himself under attack as both a psychiatrist and an ordinary person?

8   What do you think is the nature of Alan's relationship with Jill?

9   How realistic is the depth of Dysart's involvement with the case of Alan Strang?

Act 1, scenes 17 to 21

46 *The Gorbals*   poor area of Glasgow.

   kirk   Scottish word for church.

   Doric   style of classical Greek architecture.

   Zeus   in Greek mythology, chief of the gods.

51 *Horse and rider shall be one beast?*   this is a reference to Act 1, scene 7, to something Alan's mother remembers telling him in his childhood: 'when Christian cavalry first appeared in the New World, the pagans thought horse and rider was one person . . . They thought it must be a god.'

   Holy of Holies   allusion to the holiest part of the temple where only the high priest is allowed.

55 *The Ark of the Manbit*   another parody bringing to mind the Ark of the Covenant in the Old Testament; this was the chest containing the Ten Commandments as given to Moses by God.

57 *His neck comes out of my body.*   to Alan this means the unification of himself with the horse. It is also, however, a startling and somewhat surreal phallic image. It reinforces the sexual suggestiveness of the whole scene in which religious and sexual fervour become bizarrely intertwined. On page 56 Dysart instructs Alan: 'Do it, then. Mount him.' This illustrates the sexual ambiguity of the whole scene with the play on meanings of the word 'mount'. Likewise when Dysart instructs Alan to 'Ride away now' the audience cannot help but be aware of the popular meaning of the phrase 'to ride' meaning to have sexual intercourse.

   The Hosts of Hoover . . . tribe!   it is significant that Alan sees the emblems of the consumer world of electrical goods as being the enemies of his god. The implication is that the materialism of the modern industrial world is at least partly responsible for alienating humanity from its innate need for a spiritual world.

1 Who is in charge during scene 17 – Alan Strang or Martin Dysart? How do such confrontations serve to erode Dysart's faith in himself?

2 What reasons does Dysart give Hesther for the breakdown of his marriage?

3 Is Hesther ever given more than the role of simply being a passive listener?

4 What reasons might Shaffer have had for getting Dysart to consider what we mean by 'normal' in our society at this point in the play?

5 What is Dysart's attitude towards 'the normal'?

6 What part do the horses and the Chorus play in bringing Act 1 to a dramatic conclusion?

7 How does Alan's riding combine his sexual and religious obsessions?

Act 2, scenes 22 to 27

64 *a con trick*   confidence trick in which a crook robs his victim by firstly gaining their trust in order to carry out the theft. Ironically, Alan's view of psychiatry is probably one that Dysart shares with him.

65 *placebo*   medicine given to a patient to humour him. It is perhaps significant in its implication that Dysart feels his medical skills are also a fake.

67 *Peloponnese*   peninsula forming the southern part of Greece.

Kao-Pectate   medicine for diarrhoea.

68 *Dionysus*   the Greek god of fertility, and in ancient times the central figure of some of the most passionate and violent sexual rituals.

74 *without a bean*   (colloquial) having no money.

---

1   In what ways does the opening scene of Act 2 recall the play's very first scene?

2   How successful is this opening scene in re-starting the play's momentum?

3   Does Dora's outburst on page 62 alter our views of Alan and his motivations for his crime?

4   How, despite his apparent antagonism, does Alan show that he trusts Dysart and that he still needs his help?

5   How successfully do these scenes combine revelations about both Strang and Dysart? In whom are you most interested?

Act 2, scenes 28 to 35

76 *skinflick*   sex film. It suggests the kind of film in which the main interest would be centred upon the sexual activity of its stars.

   all those heavy Swedes   in the 1950s Sweden got a reputation for being more free sexually than the rest of Europe. Many sex films were made there.

90 *The Lord thy God is a Jealous God*   Jehovah, the God of the Old Testament, is portrayed as being a much more authoritarian and vengeful figure than the gentler, forgiving God of the New Testament. The 'god' which Alan has created for himself has its roots in the influences he has received from his mother's Bible readings.

93 *the odd fifty p on the gee-gees*   an occasional bet of a trifling amount on a horse race.

1   How convincing is Shaffer's portrait of Jill as an open and warm young woman?

2   How do these scenes show that Alan is still unwilling to 'grow up' and take responsibility for his own sexuality as a man?

3   The scene where Alan meets his father at the pictures borders on being farcical. Does this crude piece of humour have any point beyond serving to relieve the dramatic tension?

4   What does Alan realise that he has in common with his father?

5   How does the final scene succeed in providing a climax greater than the earlier scene where Alan blinds the horses?

▨ Study programme

The play's structure

1 Draw a flow-chart of the sequence of information which Peter Shaffer uses to tell the audience the roots of Alan's problems. The flow-chart might begin like this:

blinds six horses (page 4)
↓
'Ek' is Alan's special word (page 10)
↓
the importance of horses in his childhood (page 14)
↓
first encounter with a horse (page 22)

2 Use the information gained from the flow-chart to draw a time-line of the main events in Alan's life from his early childhood to the blinding of the horses. Part of the time-line might look like this:

Age 6: sees horse on beach and rides it

Age 7: mother reads to him over and over again from a book about horses. . .

Age 12: buys religious picture depicting Christ on Calvary

Age 13: father throws out picture and gives him a replacement picture of a white horse. . .

3 Now consider these questions and answer them in the form of an essay:

- What is the effect of Shaffer's dramatic method of cutting up and re-ordering the chronology of Alan's story?
- How successful is Shaffer in keeping the audience's interest in the 'story' of the play?

Staging the play

Peter Shaffer lays great emphasis upon the actual physical setting for the play.

☐ Re-read Shaffer's notes on the set design for this play. Then try to make a sketch plan of the set according to his requirements. Points to consider are:

- Which type of theatre would you use: the traditional proscenium arch or the more modern theatre-in-the-round? (Research each type of theatre.)
- What would be the advantages and disadvantages of each type of theatre?
- What dimensions would the set be?
- Where would you place the audience?
- What kind of lighting effects are you trying to create?
- What improvements or modifications would you make to Shaffer's original set requirements?

☐ Having completed Assignment 1 above, discuss the following:

- What problems did you face in trying to interpret Shaffer's requirements?
- Why do you think that Shaffer is so precise in outlining the set design? What effects is he trying to achieve?
- Why does Shaffer want the audience to sit as if they were at a 'dissecting theatre'?
- Why does Shaffer require the cast of **Equus** to sit 'on the stage the entire evening'?
- Which type of theatre would be the best setting for this play? Present your conclusions in a seminar paper or essay.

Character and relationships

As the play progresses, it becomes increasingly clear that Dysart's roles as both a man and a psychiatrist are being put on trial by the playwright. The process begins at the play's very outset when Dysart considers the way in which contact with Alan has made him question his work as a psychiatrist:

> *In a way, it has nothing to do with this boy. The doubts have been there for years, piling up steadily in this dreary place. It's only the extremity of this case that's made them active. I know that.*

Act 1, scene 1

Alan's *worship*, his crime, his motives for it and his behaviour all undermine Dysart's faith in himself as a doctor and as a man. Shaffer dramatises this interrogation of Dysart throughout the play, starting with instances like this exchange:

DYSART . . . *Do you dream often?*
ALAN *Do you?*
DYSART *It's my job to ask the questions. Yours to answer them.*
ALAN *Says who?*

Act 1, scene 9

The doctor's case notes

1 In order to explore the process by which Dysart comes to understand *how he can cure Alan and the consequences* of such a cure, write some of the entries which he would have made in his case notes on Alan.

Choose three or four key scenes where Dysart and Alan talk. Re-read them and then write Dysart's record of each session and his observations about his patient.

The doctor's diary

2 The play's focus is as much on Dysart the man as Dysart the psychiatrist.

In order to explore Dysart's inner life, write entries in his diary which coincide with the occasions when he saw Alan Strang. It will be important here to show how treating Alan affects Dysart in the most profound ways.

3 Shaffer has written this about the human condition:

> Man squeezed like a nut between an ideal choice and a practical one and cracked in bits . . . must always be new and painful.

Write a commentary on Dysart's case notes and his diary to illustrate his 'ideal choice' and his 'practical choice'.

The writer's intentions

In a personal essay on the writing of **Equus,** Peter Shaffer has this to say about his intentions:

> It is my object to tell tales; to conjure the spectres of horror and happiness, and fill other heads with the images which have haunted my own. My desire, I suppose, is to perturb and make gasp; to please and make laugh, to surprise.

In this same essay he describes how the play 'as it grew under my hands, came more and more to question the uses of psychiatry'.

1 Prepare to interview Peter Shaffer about his intentions in writing this play.

First, brainstorm on paper what you think he was trying to achieve. Then use these ideas to formulate questions which could be put to the writer. For example, you might choose to focus upon the character of Alan Strang and the writer's attitude to him. Questions such as: 'What impression did you intend the audience to form of Alan at the beginning of the play?' or 'To what extent is Alan's crime explicable in terms of his parents' influence upon him?' should elicit interesting answers.

Once you have found a focus for your questions you should

research your own answers by re-reading parts of the play again and noting down what you think Shaffer's answers might be.

Working in a group, take this a stage further by taking it in turns to role play the writer and improvise his answers. It is important to pause regularly to reflect upon the writer's answers and to ensure that there is solid evidence in the text of the play to support them.

Themes

A modern citizen

One of the central themes of the play is the spiritual and moral vacuum in which twentieth-century western humanity exists. Human beings' alienation from any sense of overall purpose in life is most profoundly experienced, in the view of many, by working-class, undereducated youngsters living in the industrialised west.

▣ Compare this extract from **Kes** by Barry Hines with Dysart's evaluation of Alan in **Equus**:

> ... What else has he got? [apart from his horse-worship] Think about him. He can hardly read. He knows no physics or engineering to make the world real for him. No paintings to show him how others have enjoyed it. No music except television jingles. No history except tales from a desperate mother. No friends. Not one kid to give him a joke, or make him know himself more moderately. He's a modern citizen for whom society doesn't exist . . .

Act 2, scene 25

In this scene from **Kes** the headmaster is about to cane a group of boys for smoking. This is part of what he says to them before dealing out the punishment:

> I've taught in this city for over thirty-five years now; many of your parents were pupils under me in the old city schools before this estate was built; and I'm certain that in all those years I have never encountered a generation as difficult to handle as this one. I thought I understood young people, I should

be able to with all my experience, yet there's something happening today that's frightening, that makes me feel it's all been a waste of time ... You're not interested. Nobody can tell you anything, can they, Macdowall? You know it all, you young people, you think you're so sophisticated with all your gear and your music. But the trouble is, it's superficial, just a sheen with nothing worthwhile or solid underneath. As far as I can see there's been no advance at all in discipline, decency, manners or morals ...

Kes, Penguin, 1969

How does this account of the youth of today compare with the one from **Equus**? Where do the similarities and the differences lie? Present your conclusions as a seminar paper or essay.

2 Compare the headmaster's disillusionment with his professional role with Dysart's loss of faith in his work as a psychiatrist. Do both men feel that they are failing for similar reasons? Present your conclusion as a seminar paper.

Collecting relevant quotations

A very effective way to build up a set of revision resources or notes on the play is to collect quotations under different headings.

Either write out your quotations using one page of an exercise book per heading, or use record cards. Record cards are easier to shuffle about and can slip into your pocket for instant revision sessions.

Test fellow students by reading out quotations and trying to assign to each a speaker and theme(s).

Principal characters

1 One obvious set of headings concerns the principal characters. You should note down things said by characters which are particularly revealing about themselves and also comments made by other characters about them. For example, under *Dysart* you might put this quotation:

You see, I'm lost. What use, I should be asking, are questions like these to an overworked psychiatrist in a provincial hospital? . . .

Act 1, scene 1

You might also choose to note this comment from Hesther because of the insight it gives the audience into Dysart's family life (or lack of it):

You have no children, have you?

Act 1, scene 18

Themes

2️⃣ In a similar way, collect quotations for different thematic headings. Try brainstorming ones which are appropriate to **Equus**. Some suggestions are psychiatry; sexuality; religion; family life; people's search for meaning in life; materialism; passion; horses.

This is a good way to put into a sharper focus your ideas about the play.

Beyond the play

The trial of Alan Strang

1️⃣ In Act 1, scene 2, Hesther tells Dysart:

My bench wanted to send the boy to prison. For life, if they could manage it. It took me two hours solid arguing to get him sent to you instead.

In order to explore Alan's character, the motivation behind his crime and the degree to which he can be held responsible for it, re-enact his trial.

You will need to decide who is to take on the roles of the characters in the play, and who will be the prosecuting and defending lawyers, and the judge. Hesther is one of a panel of judges or magistrates. You will also have to decide whether you are going to allow Martin Dysart to submit evidence (because in the actual play Alan is brought to him *after* his trial).

Each character will have to be researched by the student taking that role. This means tracking the character through the play and collecting anything they say which is relevant to the case. You will find the notes made for 'Collecting relevant quotations', assignments 1 and 2 on pages 110–11, very useful for this. The prosecuting and defending lawyers will face the task of presenting their cases and they will have to call each character as a witness.

Study questions

Many of the activities you have already completed will help you to answer the following questions. Before you begin to write, consider these points about essay writing:

- Analyse what the question is asking. Do this by circling key words or phrases in red ink and numbering each part.
- Use each part of the question to 'brainstorm' ideas and references to the play which you think are relevant to the answer.
- Decide on the order in which you are going to tackle the parts of the question. It may help you to draw a flow-diagram of the parts so that you can see which aspects of the question are linked.
- Organise your ideas and quotations into sections to fit your flow-diagram. You can do this by placing notes in columns under the various headings.
- Write a first draft of your essay. Do not concern yourself too much with paragraphing and so on; just aim to get your ideas down on paper and do not be too critical of what you write.
- Redraft as many times as you need, ensuring all the time that;
  - each paragraph addresses the question;
  - each paragraph addresses a new part of the question, or at least develops a part;

– you have an opening and closing paragraph which are clear and linked to the question set;
– you have checked for spelling and grammatical errors.

1 Is **Equus** a play about religion, sexuality or a mixture of both these themes?

2 Peter Shaffer has written that in writing **Equus** he came 'more and more to question the ultimate uses of psychiatry'.

Show how, through the character of Dysart, the play questions the purposes and the value of psychiatry.

3 'The violence of the action and the play's language cannot be justified.'

To what extent can you agree with this comment on **Equus**?

4 'If the diagnosis is dubious and the clinical analysis over-heated, it is perhaps less important than the opportunity it gives Mr Shaffer to provide some stunning dramatic effects.'

What are the elements in **Equus** which make it a dramatic play for an audience to watch?

5 Show the stages which Dysart goes through in his dilemma about how he should 'treat' Alan Strang.

6 How much does visual action contribute to the power of **Equus** as a piece of theatre?

7 Write about the importance of any two of the following characters: Frank Strang; Dora Strang; Hesther Salomon; Jill Mason.

8 Who is the play's central character: Alan Strang or Martin Dysart? Give reasons for your answer.

9 To what extent has Shaffer succeeded in presenting the minor characters as real people rather than types?

10 Show how the shock of Alan Strang's crime is precisely calculated, and how the play is structured to continue to produce shocks and surprises to its very close.

11 Discuss the importance of the human need for 'worship' and religious ritual in the play.

12 How important is the psychiatric setting to the play's meaning?

Suggestions for further reading

Other plays by Peter Shaffer

Five Finger Exercise (1958)
A young German student arrives in England to tutor a fourteen-year old girl. At first he fits in well with the middle-class family but then he becomes the scapegoat for the whole family's problems. Accused of trying to make love to the wife, he unsuccessfully attempts suicide.

The Royal Hunt of the Sun (1964)
Pizarro leads an army of conquistadors to Peru to conquer the golden kingdom of the Incas. A strange bond develops between Pizarro and the young Inca king.

Black Comedy (1965)
The action takes place in the apartment of a struggling young sculptor and his girlfriend, who are expecting dinner guests. The play relies upon an overriding theatrical joke: when a fuse blows plunging the flat into 'darkness' the stage is flooded with light and the characters grope about in full view of the audience.

The Battle of Shrivings (1970)
A play which in its final form has never been acted. It is in essence a dialogue on the theme of human aggression. Into the world of Gideon

Petrie, a philanthropist, bursts one of his ex-pupils to challenge him to a duel to settle a philosophical argument.

Amadeus (1979)

The play opens with whispered voices gossiping about Salieri's claim to have murdered Mozart. Having met an aged Salieri, the action then moves back in time to show the threat posed to Salieri by the highly praised and young Mozart. Salieri decides to destroy Mozart and his career.

Yonadab (1985)

Based on an Old Testament episode from the Book of Samuel, Yonadab – main character and narrator – has an incestuous love for his cousin. For this he suffers a terrible punishment and in the process renounces all religious beliefs.

Whom Do I Have the Honour of Addressing? (1989)

A one-character comedy for radio in which a middle-aged woman dictates onto tape a final desperate statement concerning her life and death. Out of a desire for self-explanation, for justice and also for revenge she sets the record straight about her relationship with the most popular film star in Hollywood.

Texts on themes related to *Equus*

One Flew Over the Cuckoo's Nest   by Ken Kesey

The story of a mental institution ruled by Nurse Ratched on behalf of the all-powerful combine. Into this terrifying, grey world comes Randle T. McMurphy, a brawling, gambling man, who wages total war on behalf of his cowed fellow inmates. This is a sharp satire on the mechanised nature of modern life.

A Clockwork Orange   by Anthony Burgess

Set in the not-too-distant future, Alex is jailed because of his juvenile excesses. There he is made the subject of 'Ludovic's Technique', a chilling experiment in Reclamation Treatment. The reader is constantly challenged to decide whether the book is horror, farce or social prophecy. Whatever it is, it is a penetrating study of human choice between good and evil.

Zigger Zagger   by Peter Terson

This is a play for a large cast and is roughly contemporary with **Equus**. It centres on a teenage boy who finds meaning in his life through being a football fan. Following his team becomes almost as much a religion with him as horses are for Alan Strang.

The French Lieutenant's Woman   by John Fowles

A novel, first published in 1969, which is interesting for its treatment of the sexually liberated individual within a repressive Victorian society and also for its use of the 'story within the story' technique. It tells in gripping style the story of a woman whose tale of seduction and desertion lures the hero, Charles Smithson, into changing his life to devastating effect.

Wider reading assignments

1. Compare and contrast Alan Strang with one or more of the central characters from the texts outlined above. How do the attitudes of their authors differ towards these characters?

2. With reference to at least one of the texts listed in 'Suggestions for further reading' and to **Equus**, discuss the extent to which the main characters are shown to be trapped by social forces beyond their control.

3. 'All of these texts challenge the reader to re-define his/her concept of what it means to be *normal* in our society.'

   Discuss this comment with reference to **Equus** and to one or more of the texts outlined above.

4. 'Peter Shaffer's plays are repeated variations of the theme of man's struggle for meaning in a world in which death dominates and religion holds no salvation.'

   With reference to **Equus** and at least one other play by Peter Shaffer, discuss the extent to which this statement can be justified.

5 With reference to **Equus, The Royal Hunt of the Sun** and/or **Amadeus,** compare and contrast the ways in which Peter Shaffer depicts the relationship between each play's central characters.

6 'Spectacle, ritual and universal themes are central to Shaffer's work as a dramatist.'

To what extent is this a fair description of the plays you have read by Peter Shaffer?

New Century Readers
Post-1914 Contemporary Fiction

Nina Bawden **Granny the Pag** 0 582 32847 0
The Real Plato Jones 0 582 29254 9
Marjorie Darke **A Question of Courage** 0 582 25395 0
Berlie Doherty **Daughter of the Sea** 0 582 32845 4
The Snake-stone 0 582 31764 9
Josephine Feeney **My Family and other Natural Disasters** 0 582 29262 X
Anne Fine **The Tulip Touch** 0 582 31941 2
Flour Babies 0 582 29259 X
A Pack of Liars 0 582 29257 3
The Book of the Banshee 0 582 29258 1
Madame Doubtfire 0 582 29261 1
Step by Wicked Step 0 582 29251 4
Goggle Eyes 0 582 29260 3
Lesley Howarth **Maphead** 0 582 29255 7
George Layton **A Northern Childhood** 0 582 25404 3
Joan Lingard **Lizzie's Leaving** 0 582 32846 2
Night Fires 0 582 31967 6
Michelle Magorian **Goodnight Mister Tom** 0 582 31965 X
Beverley Naidoo **Journey to Jo'burg** 0 582 25402 7
Andrew Norriss **Aquila** 0 582 36419 1
Catherine Sefton **Along a Lonely Road** 0 582 29256 5
Robert Swindells **A Serpent's Tooth** 0 582 31966 8
Follow a Shadow 0 582 31968 4
Robert Westall **Urn Burial** 0 582 31964 1

Post-1914 Poetry

edited by Celeste Flower **Poems 1** 0 582 25400 0
collected by John Agard **Poems in my Earphone** 0 582 22587 6

Post-1914 Plays

Ad de Bont **Mirad, a Boy from Bosnia** 0 582 24949 X
Anne Fine **Bill's New Frock** 0 582 09556 5
Nigel Hinton **Collision Course** 0 582 09555 7
Tony Robinson **Maid Marian and her Merry Men** 0 582 09554 9
Kaye Umansky **The Fwog Prince** 0 582 10156 5

Pre-1914

Charles Dickens **Oliver Twist** 0 582 28729 4
various writers **Twisters: stories from other centuries** 0 582 29253 0

Pearson Education Limited
Edinburgh Gate, Harlow,
Essex, CM20 2JE, England
and Associated Companies throughout the World.

This educational edition © Longman Group UK Limited 1993
This edition first published in the Longman Literature series 1993 in
association with André Deutsch Limited

First published 1993
Twentieth impression 2009

Editorial material set in 10/12 point Gill Sans Light
Printed in Malaysia, PA

ISBN 978-0-582-09712-4

Acknowledgements

Cover illustration by Ian Pollock

Consultant: Geoff Barton